"BEWARE OF THE FURROW THAT SHINES"

To my beloved granddaughter
Lindsay A. Hooper, B.A. (1967-1990)
who would have written it for me.

"BEWARE OF THE FURROW THAT SHINES"

— ED GIFFORD, PRAIRIE PIONEER

by

Jna Gifford Van Dyck

MATRIX
PRODUCTIONS

First printing 1998
Second printing 2001

Cover photo: Gifford Homestead, Harris, Saskatchewan

Canadian Cataloguing in Publication Data
Van Dyck, Ina Gifford, 1916-
Beware of the Furrow that Shines

ISBN 0-9688756-0-2

1. Van Dyck, Ina Gifford, 1916-   2. Frontier and pioneer life — Saskatchewan — Harris Region.   3. Harris Region (Sask.) — Biography.   I. Title.
FC3545.H36Z49 2001   971.24'2   C2001-900524-5
F1074.H36V35 2001

Design and Book Production:
    Matrix Productions Limited
    www.selfpublishyourbook.com
Back cover photo: Ollan Delany

Matrix Productions Limited
160 Water Street,
Uxbridge, Ontario
Canada L9P 1J1

Contents

Family photographs   *opposite page 82*

Ina's Family

Father – Edward (Ed) Gifford – 1885-1959
Mother – Isabelle (Isabel) Elder – 1890-1931

Maternal Grandparents
John Elder – 1854-1930
Elizabeth Elder – 1855-1930

Paternal Grandparents
Henry Gifford – 1828-1910
Kezia Gifford – 1845-1938

Sisters
Jean Elizabeth – 1914-1986
Lois Isabel – 1918-1998
Eva Marjory – 1920-1974
Iris Isabel – 1931-

Aunt
Harriet (Hat) – 1870-1958

Cousin
Wallace MacKay – 1905-2000

Brothers
Edward James (Ted) – 1922-1970
John Elder – 1923-

Aunts
Agnes (Scotland) – 1886-1950
Janet (Ettie) – 1895-1987
Elizabeth (Bessie) – 1892-1923

Uncles
John Jr. – 1885-1969
James (Jim/Jimmy) – 1888-1979

Introduction

There was once a television show that was known for a succinct phrase: 'The facts m'am, just the facts.' My stories deal only with facts! The fact is that I lived the first nineteen years of my life, 1916-1935, on the prairie farm where I was born, sixteen miles north-west of our nearest town, Harris, Saskatchewan.

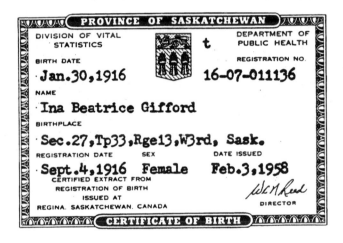

This copy of my birth certificate verifies my birthplace; the abbreviations read as follows: Section; Township; Range; west of the Third Meridian. The initiated will know what that really means: a shack on the prairie. It also means that I belong to the first generation of true prairie people; our parents had come as settlers from elsewhere.

My maternal grandparents, John and Elizabeth Elder, accompanied by their five children, age 10 to 20, immigrated to Saskatchewan from Scotland in the Spring of 1905. My father, Edward Blake Gifford, left his brother's home in Boston at age 24 and took out a homestead five miles north-west of the Elders in 1909. The letter the Canadian Government sent him about settlement in the west is terse, and the map on the back is somewhat misleading. Like most young bucks who homesteaded on the prairie, my father's intention was to make his pile and get out. But it didn't work out quite like that, at least for him.

When my grandparents reached the settlement of Saskatoon in March, 1905, the Land Titles Office was a hive of activity and of course the best land went first and fast. I have a copy of a letter my grandfather wrote to his sister Helen in Scotland, telling her of walking seventy miles south-west from Saskatoon to locate his homestead; an educated man (and a good walker!), it is a graphic record!

Homesteads of 160 acres (a quarter section) could be taken out by males eighteen or over. They were also given a pre-emption on another quarter, usually adjoining, which they could claim after the required term of continual residence. A half-section was about the maximum that could be farmed by horsepower or by oxen. I have an old photo of my mother and her sisters on a binder pulled by oxen. Their job was to keep prodding the animals with a sharp stick to keep them moving. Horses would not have needed the sharp-stick treatment, but horses were hard to come by (most were brought in from Ontario), and were very costly; old bills-of-sale for horses bought by my father and the Elders show that.

The first three years for the Elder family were particularly rough. Until the CNR line went through from Saskatoon to Calgary in 1908, everything had to be brought in by horse or oxen from Saskatoon. With the advent of the railway, homesteaders progressed from settlers to farmers. The necessities of life: coal, building supplies, machinery and the joys of the Eaton catalogue were now at hand.

My father, a fine carpenter, eventually built a big barn on a high hill and extended the original wood shack as the family of children expanded to six, a modest number in the days when families often boasted ten or eleven. But then, when the youngest, John, was just eight, my parents had an after-thought baby, Iris. Tragedy struck; our mother died in the Rosetown hospital when the baby was nineteen days old. Child-bed Fever it was called and it killed many mothers in the pre-antibiotic era. Jean, the eldest, soon left home, so at age sixteen I had five younger brothers and sisters to care for, including the baby. Our father was traumatized by the loss of his beloved 'Tot,' as he called our mother. The vaunted compassion of the prairie people did not materialize for us. There were several reasons for that: my father, proudly independent, did not enjoy a good rapport with his neighbours; it was 1931 and they had their own problems of drought and depression. One dear neighbour, Hilda Dewar, brought milk for the baby when our cow went dry. I took my instructions for the baby's care from Dr. George in Harris by phone, that is until the municipality decided we could no longer have the use of the phone because the phone bill was overdue. Our distraught father, who admitted he did not want us, abandoned his family one winter but a neighbour found him and brought him home.

Grandpa and Grandma Elder had both died in 1930, the year before the death of our mother. Her younger sister, Aunt Ettie, who had not married, offered to take the baby but our father demurred. Instead, in 1939, after he was gone from the farm, he sent Iris, alone at age seven, to live with someone he had never met, Aunt Agnes in Scotland. (Agnes, our mother's eldest sister, had not come with the others to Canada.) Iris, now a grandmother, visits Canada on her Canadian passport, but is solidly a Scot.

So, while this is an account of life on a horsepower farm on the prairies, it has a dimension over and beyond the trials and tribulations of prairie wheat farmers; the loss of our extraordinary mother who was referred to by the community as "The First Lady of the Land." I have one compelling reason for writing about our pioneer life: most of what I have read about that era has been written by people such as the local newspaper editor or school teacher. I will write from the experience of a dirt-farmer's daughter who walked behind a breaking plow and who remembers the sound of the roots of the wild prairie roses protesting their uprooting. I earned the right to be put on record by the sweat of my brow. I write from my own experience and memory; no hearsay, no input from any other. My sister, Lois, who now lives in Vancouver, paid tribute to this when she said, after reading excerpts, "Oh, Ina, it's so true."

Please enjoy.

P.S. When the breaking plow bit into the virgin prairie soil it turned a long furrow that was compact and rich with roots and fibre. If the furrow shone with dampness, the hot sun would bake it rock hard, making it difficult to till. Hence my father's advice: "Beware of the furrow that shines."

Time and Place

The basic requirement of a narrative is a sense of Time and Place. The Time of my narrative embraces the span from 1905, when my mother and her family came from Scotland, to 1935, when I left the farm. The Place was chosen by my father. When my father, Edward Blake Gifford, age 24, got to the central part of Saskatchewan in 1909, from Boston, most of the choicest land had been taken by the earlier homesteaders, like my Scots grandfather, John Elder, and his two sons, John and James.

My father's farm was five miles north-west of the Elders' and their flat land had convoluted into what was known as rolling; our half section even boasted a few steep hills. My father had tried using a cumbersome steam engine (a straw-burner), but it was not powerful enough to negotiate the hills, so he settled for horses, as most farmers did. During the time of his tenure on Sec. 27, Tp33, Rge 13, W3rd, from 1909 to 1938, he farmed only with horses. By 1938, the horse had become almost obsolete, kept mostly for use in the winter; the gasoline engine had become king. That fact makes my life-span on the farm almost historic: it covered the transition from the small farm that nurtured livestock and large families, to the vast acreages worked by equally vast machinery that required few workers. One farmer, still in our area, told me a few years ago that he, his son-in-law and a grandson, tilled an acreage that had once sustained eight families. Their large farm had no livestock, (the snowmobile had replaced the winter horse!) so there was nothing to prevent them from enjoying kinder climes than Saskatchewan's in the winter. So, in my time, I saw the transition of the family farm into big business, with the equally big loss of the human touch.

I'll never know how, or why, my father chose his farm site; it didn't make sense, was almost quixotic. The site was half a mile from the road allowance on the east, so we had to follow a winding trail, up a steep hill, to our buildings. Naturally, the municipality did not maintain farm trails, so the condition of that particular piece of road was at the mercy of the seasons' rainfall or snowfall. On the west side, the half mile trail to the other designated road allowance suffered the same lack of maintenance. That west trail was the first part of the two and a quarter miles to our school, 'up hill and down dale.'

Not only were our farm buildings awkward to reach from the main roads, they were situated slap-bang on the line that divided the two half-sections: my father's and his sister's. Slap-bang is not entirely correct as our house was actually only about twelve feet inside our line, so many of our amenities, the ash pile, the big slough, the clothes line, the garden, the tennis court, encroached on Aunt Hat's land. While my father and his sister seldom saw eye-to-eye, there did not seem to be any animosity connected with the inexplicable placement of our farm buildings. Still, when you consider that he had three hundred and twenty acres from which to choose, space was obviously not a factor, and his choice of site seemed eccentric in the extreme.

My father had other eccentricities: he did not want any trees or shrubs around the farm site. Trees and shrubs would have made life so much more enjoyable, as windbreaks, as shade in the intense heat of the summers, as protection for the garden and fruit-bearing shrubs. But no, no trees, not even a carragana hedge. And he wanted no fences on his land, except the essential fenced pasture. Even that was awkwardly placed, a good quarter mile south of the house, as if to make everyday living as inconvenient as possible. And there was another negative aspect to the building site-placement! It was between two large alkali sloughs so, when the wind blew, we endured the full effect of the offensive odours. However, it was a weather gauge of sorts: the smell of alkali usually meant that a summer storm was brewing.

My father, who was an excellent carpenter, built quality buildings: our fine big barn on the top of the hill was cedar, with a thick cement floor. While there was a roof projection to support a tackle with which to lift fodder, no tackle was ever installed. How I used to wish that there was one so we could be spared the heat-and-dust stifling work of filling the loft with dry 'prairie wool' hay.

The granary in our yard was a show piece, built of wood, on a cement foundation, painted red and long enough to accommodate three large storage sections. There was not another like it in the country. The granary was important as play equipment on summer evenings for all the Gifford siblings. The long east side had been banked high with dirt to make the unloading of grain from the wagons easier when it was scooped into the small, high openings. We used this embankment to advantage when we played 'anti-eye-over.' A player would call "anti-eye-over" as the ball was tossed over the roof; whoever caught it would run around the north or south end and try to tag the thrower. It was a game that generated much action and screaming. I don't know if any other family played it, or if it was just a Gifford children invention. But it was fun.

The garage, beside the granary, housed the Model T Ford as well as my father's vast array of prized tools. I was his right-hand man and knew the name of every tool and its use, so I could get it for him promptly as required. In Saskatchewan, as the dry air inhibited rust, the costly tools were kept in the garage all year, even the nails in the big keg in the corner of the garage never rusted.

The imposing row of machinery was lined up south of the granary, and the pigpen for the summer occupants was south of that, well away from the house. The only building at all decrepit on our yard was the small, original barn, (where my mother, as a bride, had killed a weasel using the heel of her shoe – no small feat, as weasels are not easily killed). The old barn was used as a henhouse; it was located down the hill, north of the house.

My father did not like poultry around his barns. (The exception to this rule was late in the fall when the turkeys were killed. They would be herded into a boxstall, suspended one by one by their legs, and my father would insert a sharp penknife blade through the roof of the mouth. We then quickly plucked the flapping, dying bird.) Apparently, in the early years of their marriage, my mother had raised quite a few turkeys for pin money. After they were dressed my father took them into Harris to sell. The price the merchant offered was so small my father took them all back home. They ate so much turkey meat that winter, their appetite for it was dulled for the rest of their lives! But I always liked turkey, especially when we ate the cranky gobbler.

One summer, our parents went to Saskatoon for a few days and we were left home to do two jobs: patch the roof of the henhouse with cedar shingles and paint the kitchen. We got the roof done without falling off and breaking an arm or a leg. Painting the kitchen was fun and we tackled the job with gusto. But we had not been told to avoid getting the paint on the hinges and handles of the cupboards. Our mother probably regretted that oversight as she spent hours, using a lye solution, to remove the white paint from all the metal fittings.

The house did not have an added-on look, though that is how it evolved. The generous-sized living room had been the original prairie shack, (in which I was born). It was wood, not sod. As the family increased, two bedrooms were built on the north side and a large kitchen, that included a third bedroom, on the south. It had a together look as it nestled at the foot of the long slope west of the barn. The house was painted yellow with brown trim, until the punishing winds of the dry years removed every vestige of paint, as it did to most buildings on the prairies.

The living room walls were covered with practical brown burlap half way up; the top half was papered, as was the ceiling. Wallpaper did not come prepasted, so it was a challenge to lift the flimsy paper, well coated with hand-mixed paste, and apply the long strips to the ceiling, well above the paperer's head. Papering was usually done while the children were at school, and I can appreciate why! My father's language was always colorful and wallpapering brought out his best. I don't think my mother ever said an off-colour word in her life, and in all the years of my childhood, I cannot recall ever hearing them say a cross word, or even raising their voices, to each other.

The school teacher, George Lyon, boarded with us and had the kitchen bedroom. The rest of us squeezed in, the children sometimes four to a bed, until a cot was added for Jean. The plain wooden boards on the walls of the bedrooms were varnished: they were a haven for bedbugs, found in most prairie homes then. Every summer, my mother would ignite containers of sulphur in each bedroom, close the doors against the pungent odour, and hope that the hated bugs would be exterminated, Many were, but not all. One year, she almost exterminated the whole house when a floor in a bedroom ignited . . . close call!

A shed near the east side of the house stored the coal and the washing machine. The space between the house and the shed was where the wood for kindling was kept, protected by a north wall. Oh yes, the outhouse, it was behind the wall of the henhouse, its door facing the bitter north winds; it came complete with last season's catalogue(s), the stiff colored pages being the last to be used!

Our compact farm buildings were neat, efficient, and well

built. My father's talent for building was utilized by many of the neighbours; I don't think he had apprenticed, he just knew how. Our place on the prairie would be considered isolated today; seventy miles south-west of Saskatoon, sixteen miles north-west of the town of Harris, twenty-five miles from the larger centre, Rosetown. In the days of the horse, those were long hauls.

The time frame of my narrative encompasses a generation, 1905-35, and within that, my formative years, 1916-35. If our environment shapes us, my pragmatism was moulded by that most pragmatic of provinces, Saskatchewan.

The Elders

To a newcomer in a new land, without the benefit of accurate records, weather must be a conundrum. So it was for my grandparents who, in their fifties, with five of their children, immigrated from Scotland in 1905. Apparently, for Saskatchewan, the winters of 1905 and 1906 were benign, but my grandparents would have no way of knowing that, so, when the winter of 1907 was bitterly cold and prolonged, unpreparedness almost cost them their lives. They were still living in the sod house and providing themselves with fuel from a lake area twelve miles away. Grandpa and his son, Jim, age 19, would drive the oxen there, making many trips to haul the green poplar wood that would be their only fuel. In 1907 they had not cut sufficient for a typical Saskatchewan winter. (How could they know what was typical?) That was a hard-earned lesson they never forgot. After the Saskatoon/Calgary CNR rail line was built in 1908, fuel was no longer a concern as the finest Drumheller coal from Alberta came in by rail. The rail line brought life to the isolated community.

I have part of a letter that my grandfather, John Elder, wrote home to Scotland wherein he told of his trek across the vast prairie to locate a homestead. Any travel then would have three options; by horseback; by wagon or cart, often with oxen; or walking. My grandfather was a good walker, in the best Scottish tradition, and he was known to walk the distant seventy miles to Saskatoon for the mail. After the rail line went through, a Post Office was located at the Elder farm, Bessie being postmistress.

Not long before the youngest of the Elder children, Janet (Ettie) died in 1987, age 92, a young man quizzed her about the days of the pioneers. She said that they had reached Saskatoon in March, 1905. His next remark stunned her, he said, "Oh, you would be in time to put in a crop." She was dismayed that someone of his obvious intelligence would not realize that the Canadian prairie in 1905 required that the sod be broken and cultivated before a seed could be sown the next year, if you were lucky and worked hard.

It is interesting to note what the original settlers did not have: knowledge about their soil being paramount. The quality of the soil in Saskatchewan varied from heavy gumbo to sand, not to mention the invidious alkali. There were no weather patterns established, so they could not be forewarned that certain areas were hail country and others subject to early frost. Settling on land in western Canada was a gigantic lottery. When my grandfather checked a map in the land office in Saskatoon and asked about the squiggly line through it, he was told, "That's an Indian trail." Actually, it was the long, winding Eagle Creek over which there would be no means of crossing until substantial bridges were built.

I try to visualize my grandparents making their first journey across the vast expanse of the prairie, which would seem endless to them after the narrow confines of Scotland. Their mode of travel would be slow, by horse or oxen. Horses were a luxury and, like most scarce things, the cost almost prohibitive. I do not know how much cash flow the Elders had, but I do know that their eldest son, John Jr., stayed in Saskatoon for the first few years, where he worked on the stone buildings of the university to bring in cash. He had been old enough to take out a homestead on arrival, age 20, and he spent enough time on it each year to meet the residence requirements. His homestead adjoined his parents' property.

The Elders had been a prosperous family in Scotland. I have a picture of their large brick home, and pictures of their well-groomed family taken outside of it. Indoor photography was not feasible; not enough light! Their world had come crashing down when my grandfather, with others, was named an executor of a substantial estate. They placed the estate's monies in an investment they considered to be sound; it wasn't, and the money was lost. Though there was no legal obligation for my grandfather to replace the lost money, he felt a moral obligation to do so, and he did. As a consequence, they sold their own property, salvaged what they could, and in January 1905, lured by Government of Canada broadsides extolling the Good Life on the prairies, they set sail on the *Bavaria*, crossing the mean Atlantic at the most hazardous time of the year. My grandfather had spent the winter constructing sturdy crates of one inch lumber so the cherished household china, ornaments, pictures and books would be transported safely. My Aunt Ettie said it was a good thing that he had taken precautions because the crossing was indeed rough, and when the ship docked at Saint John in New Brunswick, the settlers' effects were simply dropped from a height onto the dock. She said that their boxes were among the few that did not break open.

Now those same effects were transported along the primitive prairie trails to their homestead where the father and sons had built the prairie cliché, a sod house. I have a picture of that house; it had 'character,' boasting an attached kitchen and glass windows! In the picture, also, are two of the essentials for survival: the tepee-like free-standing pile of drying poplar poles, used for fuel, and the big, wooden barrel for water. As there were no well-drilling rigs available, the wells had to be dug by hand, an arduous task. All tools and necessities had to be transported across the rough prairie on trails that took the 'easy way,' following the natural terrain around sloughs, large and small, skirting high hills, avoiding stoney areas and large boulders, and always aware of the gopher and badger holes that could break an animal's leg. It was a tedious, jolting ride, particularly if the weather was inclement,

The vast sweep of the prairie land had been surveyed not long before; the largest area on earth to have been surveyed at one time. Survey markers indicated where the roads would be one day and the precise boundaries of the homesteaders' properties. The foundation for a viable community had been laid,

My grandfather chose his building site a short distance east of the road allowance. It was near a big slough, the willows around it indicating fertility and an assurance of moisture. Of course, the settlers had no idea of the extremes of climate they would face: the drought that lurked in the future, the variances in snowfall, and the range of temperature, from extreme heat to extreme cold. The Canadian Government's florid brochures had made no mention of the vagaries of the weather!

I am sure the Elders must have yearned for the secure life they had enjoyed in Scotland. As other settlers arrived, a surprising number were from the 'Old Country,' so a community of affinities was established; it made for contentment. Most of their purchasing was done through catalogues, Eaton's and Simpson's, by everyone. Delivery was good, quality dependable and the prices reasonable. It was the golden years of the mail order business; the mail order catalogue was the 'Bible' of my growing-up years. It was well thumbed.

My grandparents were devout Presbyterians, but when the Methodist and Presbyterian churches joined together to form The United Church of Canada in 1925, my grandmother was a founding member. Every Sunday night, my grandfather would conduct a prayer meeting for his family. There would be Bible reading, prayers and thanks to the Almighty. I participated as a child, a privilege for which I am truly thankful.

I like to visualize in my imagination, the first bite of the walking plow into the raw prairie (not new land as it is so often described; geologically the Canadian prairie is older than the land of the Nile. It had been waiting long). I can visualize the Elder family, gathered together on that interminable landscape, bowing their heads beside the oxen and the breaking plow, as my grandfather asked God's blessing upon them and their endeavours. God did bless them, *through* their endeavours.

My grandfather established one of the most respected and prosperous farms in the land. His fruit trees and shrubs, his magnificent gardens provided vegetables, fruit, berries and flowers beyond compare. The Elders were always generous in both the products of their labours, and in their compassion for those less fortunate. They contributed, from the beginning, to the well-being of the community. They were instrumental in the building of the first Public School, Hillview, west of Eagle Creek. The two youngest Elder girls, Bessie and Ettie, had missed much schooling after leaving Scotland, so the school was an essential. My mother, who was fifteen when they immigrated, attended Hillview school, but briefly. As she had gone to High School in Edinburgh, she found that the young teacher in the new prairie school had an education no farther advanced than her own.

For years, every bushel of grain that was marketed had to be hauled the long sixteen miles over rutted wintery trails to the town of Harris. This irked my grandfather, so he started a petition to have a rail line built closer to the rich wheat-producing district. It was finally built by the CPR in the late twenties, and a siding was established one mile north of the Elder farmsite. A petition was made by the community to have it named after the Elder family, it was declined as there already was a town in Saskatchewan called Eldersley. Instead, the siding was named Bents, the name of the Elders' home in Scotland. It was a misnomer if ever there was one: 'bents' in Scotland is a strip of land between streams of running water. Apart from the distant Eagle Creek, there was no running water anywhere in that part of Saskatchewan. Bents siding soon came alive: two grain elevators; the railway station; Longworth's general store, with a generous stock of just about everything and the Post Office; a Community Centre for dances, fowl suppers, meetings and Church. It was a lively place.

Alas, the two senior Elders did not live long to enjoy it, they both died in 1930: Grandma in May and Grandpa in August. My mother, Isabel, would die an early death the year after. Aunt Bessie had predeceased all of them in 1923 when she died, age 31, of cancer.

Now there were only three left, John, Jr., Jim and Ettie. Of the five Elder children who came to Canada, my mother was the only one who married. Uncle John had apparently had a girl friend when he worked as a youth in Saskatoon, but his abode, a quarter of a mile from the 'big' house, remained a bachelor shack, unpainted, but graced by the dahlias that he planted each spring. He pampered his horses, kept no other livestock, and invested all his money in stocks and bonds; his broker treated him with great respect! He was a recluse who never attended a community function, a handsome man, a gentleman . . . he died in 1969, age 84.

Uncle Jim was gregarious, well read, somewhat improvident, and loved by all. He loved to garden and he loved flowers, particularly gladiolis. He loved people and people loved him; like his brother, he did not marry. It is rumoured that he wanted to but that his parents did not approve of his choice, and besides, they needed him to work on the land. He was more suited to be a university professor than a farmer, but he made his contribution to agriculture by cultivating registered wheat, weeding the big fields by hand. He liked to experiment with new varieties of vegetables in the productive garden and grew, from seed, ordinary onions the size of the huge Spanish variety. Everything he planted seemed to flourish;

neighbours went home from the Elders burdened with the fruit of the garden. Uncle Jim would go into Harris with armloads of gladiolis which he bestowed on his favourite ladies. He was generous to a fault and, as children, we benefitted from his largesse. Our mother was his favourite, and he came to our home often for Sunday supper. We swarmed all over him and he loved every minute of it. Uncle Jim bought us the big toboggan that we used gleefully on the high hills in winter; he bought us the bicycle that gave us the freedom to coast down the long, steep trails in summer as we took turns riding it to school. We were the envy of all our friends who did not have an Uncle Jim to spoil them.

Uncle Jim bought a big steam engine when steam engines were more of a burden than a blessing. The noise of the monstrous machine caused him to lose much of his hearing until, finally at the end, he was deaf. There is an interesting footnote to the fate of his original behemoth engine. He was working in the field when a stranger approached him and asked if he could buy a part from the old engine, Uncle Jim agreed and was paid. Next thing he knew, the whole engine was disappearing down the road. It was wartime, 1939-45, and metal was valuable for the manufacture of munitions, so some fast operator had gotten a ton of metal for the price of a part. Uncle Jim made no effort to stop the scoundrel, after all, the metal in it would be put to good use!

Uncle Jim read voraciously – literary magazines, political publications, topics such as ornithology, far over the heads, or interests, of most. He shared much of his reading material with my father. When Lady Minto, the wife of the Governor-General, undertook to compile libraries for the enjoyment of isolated Canadians, Uncle Jim had one of the Minto Libraries sent to the farm, where people who came to the Post Office could also borrow books. It was a large Library that could not be accommodated in the house, so Uncle Jim built shelves for it in an adjoining building. It was his retreat where he enjoyed his leisure, reading the wealth of fine literature that had come his way, courtesy of donors in the British Isles and Lady Minto. The story of the Lady Minto libraries seems to have disappeared as an item in Canadian lore. The Lady Minto books remained in that shed until, when he was too old to act as a guardian, insects attacked it, birds nested and cobwebs gathered. His younger sister, Aunt Ettie, who by then was old herself, protested that she wanted no part of it because, "The books did not belong to them." I exhorted her to at least carry the ones that could be salvaged into a spare bedroom in her house. She demurred until I was visiting from Ontario, and loaded up boxes myself. I kept a few: the one I have in front of me is titled *Traits and Confidences* by The Hon. Emily Lawless, publisher Methuen & Co., London, Eng. 1898. The Lady Minto bookplate indicates that it was Book No. 253 from Library No. XVIII.

After their parents died, Uncle John, then aged 45, Uncle Jim, 42 and Aunt Ettie, 35, took possession of all of the Elder land. Uncle Jim inherited the home site quarter. That fact proved to be rancorous. There is a rule that when postings are made to remote areas, three persons should not be sent; almost invariably one of those three will come to believe that the other two are conspiring against him (or her). That is the way it evolved for the three Elder siblings; Uncle John and Aunt Ettie against Uncle Jim. No wonder Uncle Jim beat a retreat by going deaf! The original sod house had been sheathed with lumber and continued as the home house until the fifties, when Aunt Ettie insisted on having a new house. Grandma had wanted a new house, too, long before, and the basement for it had been poured when, lo, frost struck and the dream of a new house that year died with the stricken crop. The gaping basement is still there today, testimony to the vagaries of prairie farming.

When the new house was built, Uncle John moved into it permanently. His beloved work horses had been sold or died; his shack bore the effects of lack of maintenance. He and Uncle Jim had twin beds in one of the bedrooms; Aunt Ettie had the other bedroom. They now had the luxury of an oil heater, and other amenities . . . including electricity! After they had taken possession of the Elder property, an interesting progression took place. Actually, it was not a progression because everything ground to a halt; it was as if the year 1930, when their parents died, became frozen in time. Nothing was improved, nothing changed, there was no deviation from the established way of doing things; the three lived out the remainder of their lives as if they were still controlled by the decisions and beliefs of their parents. The three were intelligent, well-to-do people, but their personalities seemed to preclude any individual action. Uncle John was absorbed with his portfolio of investments. Aunt Ettie stated that she was in no position to suggest any changes because the "Farm buildings are now on Jim's land."

Uncle Jim plodded along, burdened by his siblings' indifference. All three had reached a stalemate; the last of the cattle and poultry were disposed of, land was sold or rented, the walls of the well caved in, cans of drinking water had to be brought in from a neighbour. It was as though the death of their parents had provoked a small death in their children, the death of the will to conduct independent lives without the guidance of their parents. It was sad. Aunt Ettie was the most spirited of the three. A young man, Fred Head, had come to the Elder farm as a labourer through the influence of his older brother, John, who farmed in the area. John had been engaged to Bessie Elder when she became ill with cancer. Fred and Aunt Ettie became engaged after Bessie died. Grandmother was so stricken by the loss of her daughter, she implored Ettie not to marry and leave her. She said, "You will have lots of time after I am gone." Ettie heeded the plea. On one occasion when she and Fred visited Saskatoon together, he wanted to buy her an engagement ring, but practical Aunt Ettie said the money could be better spent when they had their new home. Fred had applied for, and been awarded, a virgin quarter of Hudson's Bay land, just east of our farm. He had constructed a neat little home and was living there when Grandma died. Aunt Ettie looked forward to making a home with him after her long wait. But it was not to be. Fred had become tired of waiting and had turned his eye to a new school teacher. Poor Aunt Ettie! Rumours about Fred's new interest reached her and she waited and waited for him to come to call. He did not, and the word of Fred's marriage reached her via the telephone when she listened in on the party line. By this time, she was almost past her child-bearing years, she cried and cried – her mother's injunctions had borne bitter fruit.

After Uncle John died, of a stroke, Aunt Ettie and Uncle Jim bought a house in the town of Harris, rented all their land but spent the summers in the farm house. The relationship between Uncle Jim and Aunt Ettie improved, as would be expected, after Uncle John was no longer on the scene. Aunt Ettie had always favored her handsome brother, John, over the bookish Jim. In fact, Jim had always been treated as the inferior second son by everyone, everyone but my mother. My father said he had sat at the Elders' festive table and watched as John, who sat at his father's right, had been served the choicest cut while Jim, further down the table, was given something somewhat inferior.

Uncle Jim died in June, 1979, age 91. He had been hospitalized in Rosetown after a stroke, and lived as a vegetable for a number of years. He was given wonderful care in the Rosetown hospital. At the funeral in Harris, the presiding minister was a comparative newcomer and, prior to the service, she asked my sister, Lois, to tell her something about Uncle Jim. Lois told her how much he meant to his nieces and nephews, especially when we were children. She told how generous he had been with his time, taking us to picnics and dances and to his beloved travelling Chautauqua when it visited Harris. We took turns going with him. The Chautauqua was always the highlight of our summer.

The highlight, too, of a visit to Harris with Uncle Jim was a visit to the Ice Cream Parlour and spending the money he gave us for penny candy. We adored him. Aunt Ettie listened as Lois emptied her heart in gratitude for all he had done for us and his unqualified love. She said, "I had no idea you thought so much of your Uncle Jim," and that told the whole story, that statement of Aunt Ettie's. She had said to me once that it was interesting that one brother could be so successful as compared with the other. I knew she meant Uncle John because he had the money. But I remonstrated with her, "Aunt Ettie, what do you mean? are you talking about money or how a life has been lived? If you are talking about a life, Uncle Jim is the successful one." She had not thought of that.

Of the five Elder children who came to Canada (the oldest daughter, Agnes, stayed in Scotland), my mother was the one who broke free from parental control. Before she and my father were married, when she was 22, her mother said to him, "You'll have your hands full with that one." As children, we were the conduit that kept our mother in touch with her parents: she allowed us to take turns holidaying with them in the summer. Holidaying with Grandpa and Grandma meant picking fruit and vegetables. Our holidays coincided with the ripening of the fruit, and there was much of it: currants, black and red, strawberries, raspberries, gooseberries, just one thing after another. We picked peas and shelled them, picked beans, the yellow and green, and inched them ready for canning. When we weren't working in the garden, we were pressed into water-carrying service from the back well. Canning takes a lot of water! Uncle Jim had colonies of bees that were not happy to have us invade their domain. Of course, we were very happy, when the honey was lifted from the hives, to feast on the golden riches that oozed out of the honeycombs; and, after the honey was enjoyed, we still had the chewing gum, the wax from the honeycomb, it lasted and lasted. When Aunt Ettie was elderly, we were indulging in a bit of reminiscing. I said to her, "Aunt Ettie when you invited us to spend part of our holiday with you, what you really wanted was someone to pick the berries and vegetables, didn't you?" she said, "Of course."

Our grandparents had two cookstoves, the one in the summer kitchen, where most of the canning was done, and the big cookstove in the living room. The big cookstove was of an unusual design, the ashes were removed from the side, instead of the front, a sliding cover made the ashpan accessible. This extension made a cosy place to put your feet on a cold winter day, with the added luxury of the big upholstered rocking chair to sit on (if there was no grown-up to pull rank!). The black cast-iron cookstove had a large oven door that swung out, instead of being lowered, and the whole stove was so ornate it was a work of art. Certainly, no neighbour had one to compare. A magazine for antiques showed the identical stove on its cover not many years ago. The merchants of antiques, who plunder the empty farmhouses on the prairies (often when the families are south in the winter), had tried to remove the big cookstove from the old house when Aunt Ettie and Uncle Jim lived in Harris, but it was too heavy. Finally, when Aunt Ettie was in residence alone in her new house, a personable young man drove into the yard looking for 'old stuff.' Aunt Ettie ended up selling him the big cookstove and she said she did well because she got the same for it that the Elders had paid for it originally, $20.00 ... the antique magazine had given its value as $2,000.00! I did not tell her.

Many other things of value were lost to the scavengers: they took the original family photo album from under Aunt Ettie's bed and they also took something that I had coveted, a table-model Atwater-Kent radio that was in beautiful condition. It was the Elders' first radio. A few years ago, when my sisters and I were poking through an antique shop in British Columbia, the owner told us that the best place to find antiques was on the prairies. We knew! There was another antique that surely should have been saved, but it was sold for its motor, and that was Grandpa's McLaughlin-Buick car with the isinglass curtains and its sleek, rounded lines. Grandpa loved that car, he loved 'burning up' the prairie trails; he was a real menace on the road, particularly to the horses that were afraid of cars. Grandma and Aunt Ettie refused to ride with him if he went fast, fast being about twenty miles an hour; they cramped grandpa's style! He maintained his McLaughlin-Buick in perfect condition and it sat in the garage for years before it was finally desecrated. By then he was long gone. I wonder what the buyer paid for the motor?

Not everything was lost to scavengers: I salvaged a dainty white cream and sugar that had been brought from Scotland. It was Wedgwood. When Lord Wedgwood was in Toronto in 1981, I showed it to him. He said it would have belonged to their 1860 era when Wedgwood had made some plain white china but that he had never seen another like it. Lord Wedgwood was intrigued by the fact that it had survived the rigours of the arduous journey and that it finally ended up (intact!) in Toronto. He graciously authenticated each piece with his signature, though I had not had the effrontery to request it. Over the years, I have indulged in a certain nostalgia: framed pictures that are meaningful to the family. I have a wall of them in my bedroom, ranging from school class pictures taken in Scotland of my mother's and uncles' classes to a watercolour of elevators by Davenport (a rapidly disappearing prairie landmark that was termed by a famous architect "the only distinctive piece of Canadian architecture"). On the back of each picture I have listed relevant facts. Continuity is easily broken... I am striving to keep ours intact... my grandparent Elders would be proud!

Eating

We were a meat and potatoes type of family; as a matter of fact, every farm family was. We had no access to 'foreign' foods, no supermarkets bulging with temptations and curious-looking veggies. We lived off the land,

My mother was expert at canning, mostly with two-quart sealers filled with chicken and beef, peas and beans, boiled for hours in a large copper boiler. It was a cruel way to provide the winter's vegetables and the summer's meat. The cookstove had to be kept going full blast no matter how hot it was outside. There was no electricity so we did not even have the benefit of moving air. Of course, as happens so often in life, everything came all at once. The grain was harvested, the potatoes lifted, the garden vegetables stored, the glass quart jars of peaches and pears processed in an orgy of providing for the long winter ahead. With a family of nine to cook for (six children and three adults) our pots and pans were all large. We ate the basics, bread baked every other day, butter churned when needed, huge roasts of beef or pork, cakes baked in large pans. If the cake turned stale, it was converted into pudding by rolling it into crumbs and combining them with beaten egg whites and a bit of jam or fruit. I am sure there must have been a name for it; it was good.

In the summer, my mother's specialty was puddings, hot and cold. Not just ordinary cornstarch, vanilla or chocolate, made from scratch, but sago and tapioca. The tapioca pudding was baked in the oven with large slices of apple that turned almost transparent in the baking ... mmm, good.

As for meat, the tried and true favorite was shepherd's pie. A cold roast of beef would be divested of every shred of meat, which was put through the meat grinder with onions and seasoning; mixed with left-over gravy, it served as the foundation for a real feast when it was topped with mashed potatoes and browned in the oven. The so-called shepherd's pies we can buy today are a pale substitute for the real thing.

Head cheese was made from the meat of the pig's boiled head, as the name indicates. I liked to eat it but I did not enjoy watching my mother make it. She had a fine knack of seasoning things just right and the head cheese she made was a triumph. In retrospect, the thing that bothered me the most about making head cheese was watching her remove the pig's eyes. She also processed the beef tongues to perfection. The preparation of food from the 'raw' was a basic requirement, and a skill that had to be acquired if a family were to either eat or eat well. Our family ate well with my mother at the helm.

It was my Aunt Ettie, my mother's sister, who made the green tomato pickle I tried so hard to emulate. She gave me her recipe, told me her cooking secrets, but no matter, my green tomato pickle never tasted as good as hers. I gave up and came to the conclusion that the kettle she cooked her pickles in must have something to do with it.

When I was a child, no one ever bought pickles. The homemade variety were stored in one gallon crocks with close-fitting lids. My mother was particularly good at making chutneys, especially from rhubarb. I have no idea what she put in it, but it kept well and complemented meat dishes to perfection. The fruits for canning, peaches and pears, were shipped in by rail from British Columbia. The long journey, both in time and distance, meant that it was a stroke of sheer luck to have the cases arrive in our kitchen at the right moment for canning. I recall one year when liquid was running from the wood cases of pears, about the only thing they were good for was pear wine! My mother canned the fruit in glass quart sealers that required rubber rings for the glass lids. Metal rings were screwed down firmly after the boiling water process was completed. Tightening the metal rings was something of a hazard. The metal may have lost the ability to grip and a defective ring could be the source of serious scalding. Children were told to stay back as the sealers were being sealed.

Oatmeal porridge was a must every morning; the oatmeal was soaked overnight. There was no such thing as instant oatmeal, with all of its variations, there was just basic rolled oats. Oatmeal porridge had to be stirred, and stirred, as it cooked. The stirring spoon was easily identified, the wood was worn down to half a spoon. Stirring the porridge was a child's job and so was churning the cream for butter.

We churned about once a week, usually Saturday. The churn was a tall crock with a wooden lid that had a hole in the centre to accommodate the plunger. Sometimes butter took a lot longer to churn than we thought it should; it was a tedious arm-aching job. Our mother would often relieve the tedium by reciting poetry or telling us stories while she worked nearby. After the butter came, it was scooped out and the salt and food colouring worked into it before it was moulded into pounds. The wooden butter form was filled and the top pressed down to release the butter.

Butter making must have been in the family, because my grandmother prided herself on the quality of her butter, and so did the merchant in Harris who sold it. She found he would tell his customers they were buying Mrs. Elder's butter no matter its origin. So my grandfather carved the name 'Elder' on the butter press to authenticate the Elder origin right on the pound of butter.

The only tinned foods we bought were in fairly large containers, five and ten pound tins of syrup, five pound pails of lard and of peanut butter. (The word homogenized had not entered our lexicon, peanut butter had its oil floating on the top and had to be well mixed before use). All tins had secure lids and bale handles; their uses were legion from lunch pails to berry picking saskatoons and chokecherries.

When my father worked in the fields in the heat of summer, thirst was a concern. He would fill a syrup tin with a secure lid full of water and put a handful of rolled oats in it. That combination seemed to keep the water cooler and thus more refreshing. He would place it in the shade by a slough and bank it with earth.

We bought very little canned goods; if the truth were told, there was not much available in tins, mostly fish; salmon, pilchards, sardines. Soup was made in a very large blue enamel pot that was almost a fixture in winter on the back of the stove. When we came home from school, cold and hungry, it was pure ambrosia. Big soup bones would have been simmering all day with carrots and onions, the top golden with flecks of fat. Not crackers, just warm bread accompanied it.

Occasionally, when there was a wealth of animal fat, my mother would have a large pot of it on the stove to coincide with the bread dough which was ready to be formed into loaves. She would slice off a piece of dough about five inches long; placed in the hot fat, the dough would expand and cook to a golden sheen. We ate it at once, hot, it needed no embellishment. The loaves of bread that came out of our cookstove oven were no-nonsense large. Keeping the heat even and the right temperature for baking was an art in itself, every oven had its own temperament. The cook would soon learn with experience which was the hot side and when to rotate the loaves as required. Soot inevitably gathered around the outside of the oven and cleaning that out with a long-handled scraper was not a pleasant chore, but it had to be done to keep the oven efficient and the heat somewhat uniform. It was a child's job, scraping soot. On the far side of the oven from the firebox was the reservoir, the source of warm water, or on a baking day, hot water. In the winter snow was melted for the reservoir and in the summer slough water sufficed; it was the water we used for washing our face, hands and hair . . . soft water.

Cookstoves had a warming oven that jutted out over the top of the stove and was intended for keeping food warm. Ours had dual uses: the bread dough in its big bread pan was put up on the warming oven to rise before it was shaped into loaves; and the tin tea caddy was always kept there.

My father, at the head of the table, carved the roast or the fowl; the school teacher, George Lyon, sat at his left and the children in descending order of age toward our mother at the other end of the table. There was no bickering allowed at the table, we ate the food that was provided. Our grandparents always said grace before the meal, but we did not.

We had two things that flourished without care or cultivation, rhubarb and horseradish. My mother made great rhubarb pies in the summer, the horseradish was another matter. It grew like a weed and no matter how much of the white root we used, there always seemed to be more. Grinding horseradish was one of the low points of my summer when I was a child. The big grinder that clamped to the edge of a work table was metal with inter-changeable grinding discs. It was not possible to grind horseradish in the house, the smell (or the fine spray) made the operator of the grinder gag. We would set it up outside and do the horrid chore under protest. The argument for putting us through horseradish torture was that our father liked it with roast beef. In due course, I learned to like it, too, but that was after I could buy it in a small glass jar! I sometimes wonder if it was the combination of the metal in the grinder and the pungent root that made it so offensive to prepare. I'll never know.

Our beverage was strictly tea, strong tea made without benefit of tea bags which were not yet in common use. The Scots drank their tea straight, without cream or sugar. It would be a long while, not until I lived in the city, before I became addicted to coffee. We had the privilege on the farm of as much milk as we wished to drink, raw skim milk. But the drink we favoured as children was buttermilk, straight from the churn. The buttermilk sold in today's stores is an imposter, it should not even be called buttermilk. I wince when I look at the label.

We had a china cabinet in the corner by the dining room table, but it did not contain much china. The china that graced our table was plain white earthenware, distinctive for a small gold shamrock emblem. When I see a piece of it in an antique shop window today, I have to restrain myself from going in and buying it for old-time's sake.

My mother did not spank us very often, discipline seemed to be the province of our father, and harsh it was. On one occasion, though, my mother said to me, "I'm going to spank you," and she did, but even then, as a child of about nine, I thought it unjust. After all, I had not tried to be bad. I had been putting the clean dishes away in the china cabinet and I had to stand on a chair to reach the shelf. In this instance, I had overestimated my carrying capacity, and had underestimated the weight of the dishes: I tried to step onto the chair while carrying too many large plates. They did not all break when they slipped out of my hands, but many did. That is when my mother came down with her harsh injunction. I can understand why she would be so annoyed: new dishes had to be ordered from the catalogue or more costly ones transported from Harris; in the meantime, there would be an embarrassing shortage of plates. Which takes my memory back to the year when I conspired with my sisters to buy our mother a birthday gift; we secretly ordered a beautiful china cup and saucer for her from Eaton's, cost: 29 cents. When it came, it was even lovelier than we had hoped, with an intricate Oriental design, and the cup generous enough in size for her tea. We hid it in a drawer in our bedroom, awaiting the appropriate day, February 19th. But a few days before that, she came into our bedroom, where we were reading, closed the door, and asked if she could please have her birthday present early. We looked at her in slack-jawed surprise, then produced the treasured cup and saucer from its hiding place. She said that a neighbour had come for the mail and was staying for supper and that she needed the extra cup and saucer. And here, all along, we thought we had bought her a surprise . . . it was a truly disillusioning experience.

Of all the dishes we had, the piece I remember best was a blue striped bowl that did not warrant a second glance. But, on a certain Sunday, in a certain summer we went to church in our schoolhouse and my mother took the blue striped bowl. It was special that day; it held the water for the christening service. I do not recall who was christened, but I have never forgotten my pride that it was our bowl that held the blessed water.

The top shelf of the china cabinet harboured a few good pieces: a delicate, fluted china bowl in a cradle of silver; a tall glass pickle jar on a silver stand that also held the silver pickle fork; a dozen ornate sterling silver tea spoons that had been our mother's wedding gift from her parents (initialled IHE: Isabel Hamilton Elder). The tea spoons were finally apportioned equally as were the two twelve-piece china tea sets that the Elders brought from Scotland. It almost requires the wisdom of Solomon to make everything come out even and invariably everyone has their heart set on a particular item. I have tried to get around this dilemma by making a comprehensive list of the things in our household that have sentimental, or real, value. I gave each of our three children a copy and asked that they indicate the items they preferred. Then I had to play Solomon as I marked the master copy that shows who should get what. I know they will end up squabbling over some little thing I considered not worth listing! That is life.

I honestly don't know how we survived the years of drought and depression after our mother died. I know how we survived the second winter: our father, with his east coast background, ordered cases of salted herring and dulse, both foreign to his children's palates, but we adapted, we had no choice. I boiled the salted herring to reduce the salt content, then made a white sauce to make the fish go down. Learning to like dulse was more difficult, but in the end we were all chewing it, though I must admit I do not buy it today when I see a costly small package in the local market... I didn't like it *that* well! The two primary foods that sustained us were bread and oatmeal porridge. There was no feed for the poultry, so eggs and chicken were in short supply. One evening a couple of 'young swains' came to call and it was evident that they expected to be fed! What should we do? We did the only thing we could, we killed the rooster! He was a tough old bird, those two callers did not make a repeat visit.

It was remarkable that we did not become ill from malnutrition, or show, in later years, the effects of our restricted diet. We had one advantage over later generations: the little food we had was pure and not adulterated by additives. On the other hand, our milk was not pasteurized and real danger existed when the livestock, both horses and cattle, developed encephalitis. Our mare, Dolly, lost her twin foals, and the cows went dry. By this time, our lives had been lived in such a negative state for so long, we had become almost inured to negativity. But it was a sad loss... the colts. On a positive note: I cannot recall one neighbour who could be termed obese.

This anecdote about Eating should end on something sweet... candy! Most of our candy making was done in the winter, sometimes we would simply take the boiled candy and pour it thinly on the big, white snowbanks just outside the kitchen door, where it hardened immediately in the delicate patterns we designed.

But the most fun with candy was when we would take a big, hot piece in our well-buttered hands and start to pull with a partner. We pulled quick and hard, seeing how far we could extend it, then we would double it back and pull again and again. As the candy cooled and stretched, it became lighter and lighter in colour and hardened until we could pull it no more. We then used the scissors to cut it into bite-size pieces, after we had given it a final twirl so it resembled horehound. I always loved horehound, which we bought as a penny candy in Harris. In the stores today, they will tell you that they sell real horehound, but it is a pale imitation of the real thing.

Hallowe'en was a night for mischief and for apples. The mischief was taken care of by the young men who went from farm to farm knocking over outhouses and putting buggies on the top of barn roofs. The girls, with open mouths, bobbed for apples in a big tub of water, or we suspended them by string from the kitchen clothes line and tried to get a bit of apple without hands which we kept behind our backs. A few apples provided a lot of Hallowe'en fun. The evening would climax with a taffy pull and a ghost story by Dad.

I said I would end this anecdote with candy but I cannot omit something as memorable for me: cheese! Cheese was not made on the prairie, cheese came to us from Ontario. One cold winter night my father came home from hauling yet another load of wheat to the Harris elevator. His arrival was always greeted with eager anticipation; there might be a treat for us...usually there wasn't. This particular night he had brought a treat for everyone, a rectangular wood box about 12"x4"x4" that was lined with tinfoil to protect the golden yellow cheese inside. For me, it was a delicious introduction to the world of aged cheese. I have no idea now how old I was, but that delectable taste experience has stayed with me for all of my life. I shop now at a cheese specialty shop on Bayview Avenue in Toronto but even their 9½-year-old cheese can't compare with the piece of ambrosia that came on the sleigh that bitter winter night in Saskatchewan. I learned later that my grandfather Elder had a taste for aged cheese, so I came by it honestly. It would be interesting to know now, how much that box of cheese had cost at Bill Marshall's General Store in the early nineteen twenties.

The Pasture

Our pasture was not an ordinary pasture; it had a distinct personality of its own. When I was a child, it still bore the imprint of the original inhabitants of the prairies. Their paths criss-crossed it at random, well-worn paths that had obviously been well travelled, indicating that it was a popular site for either the aboriginal people or the herds of buffalo. I am curious about who was responsible for those paths that my feet followed. We knew that the buffalo had been there in numbers because their sun-whitened skulls still littered the unbroken pasture land. It was fun to find a buffalo skull, but the big prize was to find one that still had the horns intact. With great glee we would wrench the horns from the skull. Sadly, this illustrates our society's disregard for the past, through indifference or ignorance, or both. The pioneers were so intent on making a viable life for themselves, they paid little or no attention to the land's historic content, so it was sacrificed to the dual Gods of exigency and greed. Our casual use of a stone, which was obviously a prehistoric tool, as a plaything, illustrates an unconcern of momentous proportions. It makes me sad to think of it and I have always hoped that some day that stone would be discovered by the discerning.

There were some fairly large stones in the pasture, but none large enough to qualify as a buffalo rubbing stone. Some of the stones bore the enticing red gleam of the ruby stones that were at one time thought to be genuine rubies, a fact that caused much excitement and, I believe, the staking of ruby stone claims. It was a tempest in a teapot because it was soon established that they were just pretty red stones that reflected the light.

Our pasture differed from most farm pastures insofar as it was not adjacent to the buildings and there was no fenced access to it. That meant that the animals that were put in or taken out had to be led or herded. The entrance to the pasture was about a quarter of a mile south of the house, a long trek for a child.

Our pasture was fenced with page wire which was superior to the standard barbed wire. The wire was fastened to cedar wood posts, which had to be imported to the prairies, and the post holes were laboriously hand dug. I liked the page wire fencing; its rectangular openings were simple for a child to slip through and there were no barbs to cut flesh, or clothes. To get through a page wire fence, first you put a leg through, then your head and shoulders, the rest of you followed easily.

Two of the distinguishing things about the pasture were its gates, and thereby hangs a tale. The gates were wide enough to accommodate machinery; they were made of sturdy tubular metal and had hinges, on which they swung easily. Altogether, they were superior gates. They had been ordered from, where else?, the Eaton catalogue. Two had been ordered by my grandfather; one for himself and one for my dad. They duly arrived at the Harris railway station, but instead of the two that had been ordered, there were three. My grandfather wrote to the T. Eaton Company and asked what disposition should be made of the extra gate. Imagine his surprise when, instead of sending instructions, the company sent another gate, free of charge, with apologies for not filling the order properly. My grandfather tried again, he wrote and set out in detail what had happened and asked again what he should do with the extra gates. Once again, the company shipped another gate, free of charge. My grandfather gave up, he accepted the gratis gates and gave one to my father. That is how we came to have two deluxe gates for our pasture.

The pasture which was about a third of a mile long, was L-shaped, the base of the L extended east and ended in a big slough, a haven for waterfowl. There were two other sloughs in the pasture, the one at the south-west corner was a small extension of a big alkali slough that was on a neighbour's property; no grass grew on it. A road allowance separated the farms, but no road had been built, probably because the alkali was a deterrent. The third slough was near the entrance to the pasture. It was large, shallow and quickly dried up in the summer. Its grass was not coarse slough-grass so it was good feed for the grazing livestock. The native grassland in the whole pasture was adequate for grazing until the heat of the summer retarded its growth. That is when the gate at the far end of the pasture would be opened and the children sent to herd the cattle as they fed in a slough nearby. It was not a large slough but it maintained its water and had particularly lush grass all summer. The hungry cattle were to feed in the slough and were not supposed to get into the adjacent oat field. Theoretically, it should have been easy, but the cows much preferred the succulent green oats to the slough grass. Who could blame them?

Keeping the cows in the designated area required constant vigilance, a vigilance that interfered with our propensity to play farm; we would squat in the tall grass at the edge of the slough, clear an area, and then fashion our farmyard from mud that was easily moulded, and fast to dry. We made some great farms by the edge of that slough, using pebbles for animals.

We would become so immersed in building that it was easy to forget the wayward cows. There was a big stick hanging over our heads, however. If our father went to the south loft door, he could see what was transpiring in the slough. As we impatiently herded the cows back into their prescribed area, we kept our fingers crossed that no-one was watching from on high. Toward the end of the afternoon, we kept our eyes on the loft because the signal to put the cows back in the pasture and come home was a white cloth waving from the loft door, a welcome sight. But before we left, we gathered the broad leaves of the slough grass so we could lay them edgewise between our two thumbs and blow. We played slough-grass music all the way home,

When the cows calved, their delivery room was at the far end of the pasture. The pasture had its ups and downs, like all the rolling land on our farm. The cow about to calve would hide behind one of the steep knolls, apart from the rest of the herd. On one occasion, I came upon Bessie, just as she was calving. It was a sight my young eyes had not seen before. I stood well back and gazed in wonder as Bessie dropped her calf. Dropped was the right word as she did not lie down to have it and the poor little thing literally dropped to the hard ground. It is probably nature's way of protecting the calf, as the mother was on her feet and ready to immediately charge an enemy if necessary. A cow with a new calf is not to be trifled with; I turned and ran for home eager to spread the word that Bessie had a new calf. No one seemed perturbed that I had watched it being born. I did, however, insist on the right to name it: I called him Billy.

Billy was destined from birth to be special; he was to be our beef ring animal. Too bad for Billy that he was born a male; females were not considered worthy to be beef ring animals. Every other year, a member of the beef ring was required to provide an animal for slaughter. The community butcher was careful to apportion the meat to individual members by cut so no family would be favoured with the choicest cuts. Families would take turns delivering the meat, by horse and buggy, to their neighbours each week. As in all joint ventures, it was a matter of pride that the animal that was put in the beef ring, would be superior. So my Billy was given superior attention; the best feed, the best of everything that the farm could provide, so when his turn to be the beef ring animal finally arrived two years hence, it would be noted that the Giffords had entered a quality animal.

The beef ring butcher played favourites with us in one special way, though. The family who provided the animal for that particular week was entitled to the offal, but it was not always desired. The butcher knew the families that did not like liver, so we often found a bonus of liver in our allotted share. We ate a lot of liver when I was a child. I liked it, still do.

Back to the pasture. We milked the cows there in the summer evenings. There was a good reason for doing that even though it meant a long walk to carry the heavy pails of milk to the house for separating. The good reason? the mosquitoes! Prairie mosquitoes are renowned for their size, their viciousness and their number. They live up to their reputation. The only way we could get the cows to stand still for milking was to build a smudge that generated enough smoke to keep the mosquitoes at bay. The fuel that provided the best smudge was dried cow dung. There was plenty of that in the pasture, so we would gather it and light a smudge to prevent both man and animal from being eaten alive. Without the smudge, I have seen so many mosquitoes on Bessie's red hide, she looked grey. A hand wiped across her back would yield all the mosquitoes a hand could hold, just in one swoop. Long after the milking was over, the cows would linger in the smoke from the smudge, free for a short while from the hated mosquito menace.

My mother was smart: she never learned how to milk. If my father was away for a few days, arrangements would be made for a neighbour to do the milking. She refused to play the role of milkmaid. I don't blame her; with all the demands on her time and energy, I don't know how she could have had enough of either to milk a cow. I tried it, but it was not one of my major accomplishments for which the victim cow was no doubt grateful. She did not have to put up with my ineptness very often.

In the heat of the summer, when both horses and cattle would be in the pasture, keeping the trough full of water was a major chore. The well was not deep, about twenty feet, so filling the trough was not arduous. What was a hazard, was having to work in the midst of thirsty animals all vying for their place at the trough. It never seemed to be recognized that filling the trough in the pasture was unsafe for a child, but it had to be done, so we did it regardless. There was one particularly scarey episode when my young brother, Ted, went to the pasture to fill the trough. A maturing steer decided that he was more bull than steer and took after my brother. It turned out that the castration when the animal was a calf had not been thorough, and the steer became belligerent as only a bull can. My brother was lucky to escape with his life.

I had a pasture scare myself. It happened after our mother had died. We needed milk for the formula for the new baby and unfortunately, the summer when Iris was eight months old, we did not have a milking cow giving enough to provide our needs. A neighbour south of us had a large herd of cattle, and my father contacted him and suggested a trade. The one cow we then had was strictly a beef animal, a big cow, well fleshed, but not a milker. My father asked the neighbour if he had a cow that could give us milk; he said he had one that had just freshened and would probably be ideal. My father asked him to take our cow from the pasture (she was its lone occupant), and leave his cow there. It was done. When my father went down to the pasture to assess the new cow, he saw at a glance that he had been had. A skinny little brown cow that looked no more than a calf herself had been exchanged for our robust animal. My father should have known better. The farmer he had negotiated with was famous for his sharp deals. He certainly put one over on my dad. Later in the summer, on a hot day, I went to the pasture to fill the trough for the cow. By this time, her milk had dried up and we were borrowing milk every day from a generous neighbour who recognized our plight. The little brown cow drank her fill at the trough, as I went to leave by the gate which was about a hundred yards away, she put her head down and charged after me from the far side of the trough. She had horns and she meant business. I was terrified. I ran for the fence as though fleeing from a demon which, in a sense, I was. My agility in getting through a page wire fence stood me in good stead. I made my escape just ahead of her charge. When I looked back at the cow, I felt guilty. There she was all alone in that big, hot pasture with not even a tree for shade, or to rub against, and the isolation had no doubt made her go a bit crazy. All she wanted was company, and I was leaving. It was sad.

Every time I think of the pasture, I remember the little yellow violets that grew in a secluded area by the west fence. They were a beautiful, pure yellow, a much lovelier colour than the yellow buttercups that were common to the prairies. Years after I had left, I returned to the pasture to see if I could retrieve a few yellow violets for my city garden. Alas, the pasture land had been broken, the yellow violets were no more. Like the buffalo skulls, they had become but a memory.

Just wondering: There were buffalo skulls in the pasture, but no other buffalo bones; what happened to them?

When the cows were put in the pastures they usually headed straight for the salt lick, the big, pink block of iodized salt that was deeply grooved by their rough, licking tongues. They craved salt, to the extent that if it was not available, they would lick old whitened bones to try to get it. A neighbour's cow died from the attempt; a small bone lodged in her throat and choked her. Our mother told us, when we came home from school, that a cow had choked to death in our neighbour's nearby pasture; we went to look. Just as we approached the dead cow, bubbles oozed from her mouth and nose ... we did not linger.

Gophers

When I was a child, a homesteader's daughter, gophers were an elementary part of our prairie wildlife. They were not an attractive rodent: the dull gray of their smooth fur blended with the colour of the sere prairie grass, their short tails lacked the expressiveness of a squirrel's, their eyes were small and beady, even their ears were nondescript. True enough, gophers provided seasonal sustenance for soaring raptors and wily coyotes. Their colonies, established on knolls for easy outlook, consisted of labyrinths of underground burrows with prominent entrances and, at some distance, strategic exits. They multiplied, well, almost like rabbits and were seemingly

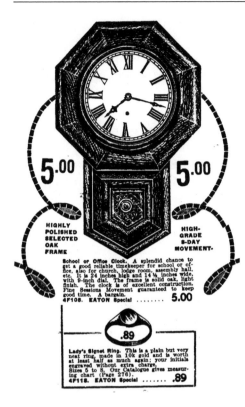

HIGHLY POLISHED SELECTED OAK FRAME

HIGH-GRADE 8-DAY MOVEMENT-

School or Office Clock. A splendid chance to get a good reliable timekeeper for school or office, also for church, lodge room, assembly hall, etc. It is 24 inches high and 14 ½ inches wide, with 9-inch dial. The frame is solid oak, light finish. The clock is of excellent construction. Fine Sessions Movement guaranteed to keep good time. A bargain.
4F108. EATON Special 5.00

Lady's Signet Ring. This is a plain but very neat ring, made in 10k gold and is worth at least half as much again; your initials engraved without extra charge. Sizes 5 to 8. Our Catalogue gives measuring chart (Page 276).
4F118. EATON Special .... .89

The clock that was watched by every school child! The ring that the one-cent gopher tails could buy.
Items offered for sale on the back of an Eaton's catalogue order form, circa 1920.

ineradicable. My father used to try: he would place small quantities of a lethal gas generating powder, Cyanigas, at the entrance to their burrows. Whether the gas worked or not, we could never be sure; dead gophers cannot be counted in their burrows.

As children, we spent many summer days pouring pails and pails of slough or well water down gopher holes after the boys had expertly arranged binder twine snares at the entrance – or was it the exit? If everything came together perfectly: water, snare, patience, dexterity and the choice of the right hole, voilà, another dead gopher and money for the tail. The going rate was a cent each. Some boys tried to cheat by cutting the tails in two before presentation to the municipal office for the payoff, but the clerks there usually knew the length of a gopher's tail. A cent a tail was serious money in the 1920's when you consider that the Eaton catalogue of the day offered a lady's 10 carat gold signet ring for 89 cents, including engraving.

My mother especially disliked gophers; they invaded her garden when her carefully tended greens were at their most succulent and I have seen her in tears over the desecration. On the dry wind swept prairie, greens were a rare treat, and, as we now know, essential to the diet of adults and children. There were six children in our family, born 1914 to 1923, and summer fare had no winter substitute; refrigerated cars were unknown on the trains that pulled into our nearest rail station, Harris, Saskatchewan, 16 miles away.

But there was one green that the gophers did not eat, it grew wild and came up early in the spring. We called it pigweed (it is also known as lamb's quarters). Pigweed had to be pulled when it was young and tender, before it developed seeds. It grew plentifully, and being a weed, it grew where it was least wanted. After being washed, boiled and slathered with home-made butter, it was sheer ambrosia; just what we needed after our long meat-and-potatoes winter. It preceded the cultivated greens from our mother's garden.

Our mother would beg our father to do something about the hated gophers as they stood cheekily on their hind legs by their burrows and dared the carnivores, both the raptors and the humans, to catch them. But, as is common in all life, there came a day.

It was a typical summer day on the prairies, threatening to be hot, bright with sunshine, not a cloud in the sky, a day in which only good things could be expected to happen. My father had left early for Harris to pick up a part for machinery that seemed to be in constant need of repair. Toward noon the sky clouded over. We had no access to weather reports, and even if there were forecasts, we would not waste the batteries of our big Marconi radio on anything as frivolous as the weather. The ubiquitous Farmers' Almanac hung in pretty well every farm kitchen, but no one in their right mind would take its year-long weather prognostications seriously.

So when the sky darkened ominously on this particular day and the strengthening wind cavorted with dust devils in our bare front yard, we assumed that a rain cloud was passing over. Rain clouds were always welcome, however brief their passing, but the rain we welcomed most was a good three day soaker to renew the subsoil moisture. This was not to be of that genre. In the beginning, the whole sky became darker and darker until even the animals and poultry became afraid. The hens hurried their chicks into the shelter of the henhouse, the dogs whined at our kitchen door to be let in, the cats took refuge in the barn hayloft. We children huddled around our mother in the kitchen and watched in fear as day seemed to turn to night. We did not have long to wait, the wind increased in fury, the rain hit, almost horizontally, with a vengeance. Our mother took action: windows and doors were closed, rags and towels were gathered to sop up the water that came in every crevice around doors and windows. The whole world seemed to turn a murky green as sheets and sheets of raging water threatened to engulf us, shatter the windows, tear the roof from our house.

It went on and on without surcease; some of the children cried in terror. The tempest made such a sound on the roof, the walls and on the ground that it was almost impossible to tell from where the sound emanated. It was like being confined in a ship's cabin in an angry sea, at least that is how our mother described it after. She would know, she and her family (five siblings and parents) had sailed on the small ship, *Bavaria*, and had crossed the treacherous Atlantic ocean to Saint John, New Brunswick, leaving their home in Scotland on February 23, 1905, the worst time of the year for the crossing. She had experienced the rage of the sea.

Finally the storm stopped, swept by us, almost as suddenly, it seemed, as it had come. At first we were afraid to venture from the house and stayed by our mother like chicks seeking the shelter of the mother hen's wings. When the sun made a sodden appearance, she told us to go and see what it looked like outside. We charged out into a world of wonder where mud, glorious mud, oozed up between the toes of our bare feet, the thickest, deepest mud we had ever seen ... there was even mud on the very top of the grassy knoll west of our house. Our big slough to the south was almost a lake and our mother said not to go near it. We darted about the farmyard exploring in wonder and ecstacy.

The pasture! What would it be like in the pasture? We splashed through the quarter mile of mud and water to see, being careful not to run through our mother's garden, where only a few green stalks stood up through the mud. At the pasture gate, we stood and gazed in amazement. Every small gully on the rolling land was now a slough with overflowing water trying to find a lower level.

But what was this in the grass? ... baseball-sized spheres of dark fur. We went through the gate and picked up one of the spheres, hesitantly, and, in keeping with the deviant day, found that it was a gopher. They were everywhere we looked, immobile, inanimate balls of wet fur. The only variance in the uniform darkness of their color was repulsive white woodticks that clung to the back of each gopher's neck.

Strangely, the gophers did not uncoil or make any protest when we picked them up to examine them. Quickly we ran to the pasture well for a battered, two-handled galvanized tub, then we placed gophers in it, layer on layer. We could hardly wait to show our mother what we had found.

We carried our heavy cargo back up to the house, taking turns on the handles; finally we set it down in triumph on the kitchen floor, the gophers still coiled as we had found them. Our mother's reaction was predictable once she realized what the tub contained, "Get those things out of here!" Gophers were no more welcome in her kitchen than they were in her garden. We understood that, but we hesitated, there was one aspect to our cargo that she surely had not grasped: we wanted to capitalize on our find. We stood our ground stubbornly, standing by the tub; could we not, we pleaded, take off the tails? Tail money would never be this easy again. But she shook her head. We tried in unison again, "Please, can't we have the tails... please?" Our mother silenced our greedy clamour with one short, telling sentence, "It wouldn't be fair."

That settled the argument, we knew about the word fair after the many injunctions we had been given to fight fair. Dolefully we lugged the tubful of still inanimate gophers back to the pasture after being told to not let them out near the garden.

Back in the pasture, we turned the tub on its side and dumped them all out. Then a strange thing happened: as they felt the earth under them they slowly uncoiled and returned to being just ordinary wet gophers. But they did not scamper away, they crawled on their bellies as though feeling their way back from oblivion, not knowing, of course, that their fate had lain in one simple sentence, "It wouldn't be fair."

We never again had an experience like it, a deluge of such intensity and volume that it drove all the gophers from their burrows and rendered them comatose. Nor have I heard of any similar occurrence.

The Garden

A large family needs a large garden. I think of our garden when I was a child as being somewhat schizophrenic, if that designation can be used for a garden. The problem was that my grandfather Elder's garden was reliable in the extreme: the pride of the district. The naturally rich soil of the garden was augmented annually with the best fertilizer obtainable, the manure from the stable. The garden was sheltered from the harsh prairie winds and the excessive heat of summer by a well-chosen shelter belt.

My Uncle Jim studied the winter's crop of seed catalogues and aspired to the best. Each spring he tilled the garden soil with a one-horse walking plow. (I understand the plow has been preserved as a pioneer artifact by the maker, The John Deere Company). My uncle's large garden was three-part, rotated each year, part vegetables, part potatoes and the other third left fallow. The permanent strawberry bed was at the south end and my grandfather's fruit orchard at the north. The orchard was my grandfather's joy.

My grandparents had an arrangement for coping with unexpected visitors: neighbours had a habit of dropping in, and they were always made welcome. My grandfather would go out to greet them and, as the horse was being tied to the hitching post, my grandfather would invite the guests to see the gardens; they readily agreed. While he was showing the orchard and garden, my grandmother would be hastily putting the house in guest-greeting order. My mother once remarked that it was amazing how much could be done in the five minutes after horses' ears were spotted coming over the hill! My grandparents had it down to a fine art. The visitors would be plied with the bounty of the garden or orchard, there was always a yield far beyond the need of the Elder family.

As I said, our garden was almost schizophrenic in comparison; it boasted no shelter belt (my father refused to plant one), any fertilizing was haphazard; my father was indifferent about its care and my mother had little time and not much desire to baby the garden. In the heat of summer, if there was still water in the nearby big slough, my father would put a barrel on the stoneboat and haul water to the garden. I don't think it helped very much, the end result was likely to be a hard crust that baked on the surface with little subsoil moisture having been added. But the garden represented work for the children, especially the potato patch. The potatoes of choice were Irish Cobblers, huge, hollow-hearted, a fact that made them poor winter keepers. The Colorado potato bugs loved them. We would be sent to the patch in July with tin cans half full of coal oil (kerosene) into which we would knock the beetles from the underside of the leaves. The young grey bugs could be easily squashed if we desired, but the adult black and yellow bugs were not so easily vanquished. Killing potato bugs was a chore we dodged if possible, it was tedious backbreaking and seemingly never-ending. And certainly, no one ever praised you for a job well done.

The first yield from the garden was always the best: the red radishes were tender and sweet, the leaf lettuce (head lettuce was an unknown) had not yet turned bitter and the new green peas were pure ambrosia. Later, the corn, carrots, parsnips and turnips came into their own. We did not seem to have much luck with cabbage and cauliflower, but I recall one year when we had a big patch of kohlrabi, a vegetable whose stem above the ground swells into an edible bulb-like formation. I liked kohlrabi, and so did the cattle. I never saw it in the supermarkets until recently when it is now being discovered, but the size is small compared with the kohlrabi we harvested when I was a child, about a third of the size. My Uncle Jim had probably discovered it hidden in his seed catalogue treasures. He was always game to try anything that could be grown from seed.

The problem with trying to grow cabbage and cauliflower was the insects that plagued them, particularly that little white cabbage moth; its ravages made the wintering of infected cabbage impossible. No chemicals were available to ward off garden destruction. It was a good year or bad depending on the weather and the pests; you planted your seeds and took your chances.

Uncle Jim, my mother's bachelor brother, was the one member of her family with whom my father had a good rapport. Uncle Jim compensated for the deficiencies of our garden with largesse from his own. He had colonies of honey bees and the bulging honeycombs from his hives were a staple of our table. We chewed the wax after enjoying the rich honey. My memories of dear, generous Uncle Jim are enriched by the memory of sweet honey: it seemed so in character that he would provide such goodness for us.

My mother never cried, well, hardly ever. I saw her cry once, about the garden. About her strawberry plants, actually. She had wanted to establish a permanent strawberry bed and Uncle Jim, had supplied her with sturdy runners from his plants that produced strawberries of gargantuan proportions, delicious, too. She planted them, with his help, at the south end of our garden plot where they could receive special care. They didn't produce much the first year but came through the winter with the promise of a good second-year crop. My father always raked the garden soil in the spring, using the wide three-section rake that he used in the fields. I can still see the unbelieving look on my mother's face as she saw that big rake demolishing her beloved strawberry patch.

There was no doubt it was deliberate. My mother never tried growing strawberries again.

We always planted flower seeds. I liked planting the big nasturtium seeds, but most were tiny like the poppies, phlox, sweet william, salpiglosses and night-scented stock. Like the vegetable garden, the success of the flowers depended upon the elements.

And like the vegetables, our flowers could never rival the flowers grown by the Elders. Their tastes were more exotic; zinnias, begonias, asters, hollyhocks, and, their specialty: every size and hue of gladiolus. My Uncle Jim would take armfuls of gladioli to the storekeepers' wives in town, to their delight and to the chagrin of his very proper mother and sisters.

My grandmother's house in early spring is a special, delightful memory. Her wizardry with bulbs gave it the scent of hyacinths, the cheery yellow and whites of daffodils and narcissuses, the shy little crocuses, all brought cheer and sweet scent to her home long before the frozen ground outside was ready to till.

But oh, it was pleasant to sit outside our home on a summer evening and smell the sweet night-scented stock; it left a lasting impression of family togetherness.

My Mother

My mother, Isabel Hamilton Elder, came from Scotland, a feisty fifteen year old, in 1905. There were seven in the Elder immigrant family: the parents, John and Elizabeth, and five children: John – age 20, James – 17, Isabel – 15, Elizabeth – 13 and Janet – 10. They travelled in a comfortless, wood-seated settlers' car on the train from Saint John, New Brunswick, where their ship had docked.

The family arrived in Saskatoon, March 1905, and my grandfather set out at once to locate a homestead. The land he settled on was stone-free, level and fertile, just what his Scots heart desired. It was located twelve miles north-west of what was eventually the town of Harris, built after the CNR line went through from Saskatoon to Calgary in 1908.

But this is about my mother. She was always full of ginger and sometimes irked by the strictures of Scottish Presbyterianism.

It didn't take her long to become engaged to a neighbour lad. He was a talented artist; I have sketches he drew of her in India ink which are lovely, and cherished. He was eighteen and his family, the Kyles, like the Elders, had taken out a homestead. Then tragedy struck: typhoid fever. Three of the boys in the Kyle family died, including my mother's love. As it was the middle of a brutal winter, no graves could be dug, so the bodies were wrapped in blankets and kept in an outdoor shed until proper graves could be prepared in the spring. Such tragedies were considered part of the homesteading life as there were no doctors to summon and little information regarding communicable diseases; you just took your chances.

But eventually love flourished again for my mother. This time he was a handsome young man who had come to a neighbour's to help with the harvest. Isabel was sure that she had found her man but, even though they became formally engaged, it was not to be. The villain was a drawstring cloth curtain that separated his upstairs sleeping quarters from that of the family's teen-age helper. The outcome was predictable: pregnancy, and a hurried shotgun wedding. Once again, my mother was heartbroken, and humiliated.

Then Ed Gifford took out a homestead, in 1909, five miles northwest of the Elders. He was a handsome young scoundrel, a travelling salesman (flour) who had left his brother's home in Boston and gone to western Canada, like so many other young men, not with the intention of staying, but to make his pile and get out. (The copy of the letter [on next page], sent to him by the Canadian Immigration Department, is a rare record of that era.) He went first to Alberta, High River and Calgary, before taking out a homestead, Section 27, Township 33, Range 13, west of the 3rd Meridian, in Saskatchewan.

For a young man from the exciting cities of the east, there was very little incentive to linger in the harsh west. But, ah, the best laid plans of mice and men, there was Isabel Elder, the belle of the district, looking for someone to call her own. They became engaged, not with the Elder family blessing: Edward Gifford was not cut from their cloth.

One lovely summer day, Isabel was visiting at Ed's farm; by this time his aged parents had joined him. Like any young girl in love, she was eagerly awaiting the day when she would be his wife. But

THOMAS HETHERINGTON
DMINION GOVERNMENT IMMIGRATION AGENT
PEOPLES NATIONAL BANK BUILDING   73 Tremont st ,
17 DUDLEY STREET   Room 202

TELEPHONE 851 ROXBURY

Boston, Mass.   April 7,1908.
ROXBURY, MASS.

Dear Sir:-

          I beg leave to say,in answer to your letter of
inquiry,that I am sending you ubder another cover some
publications relatinf to the Canadian North-West and that
I herewith enclose an application sheet to be filled out.
When you will have decided the time you will leave for
Western Canada to take up a farm send it back to me in
order that I may be in a position of forwarding you a
certificate that will allow you to travel for one cemt
a mile from M°ntreal to any settling point of Alberta,Sas
katchewan and Manitoba(west of Winnipeg.)

          If you are desirous of obtaining further in-
formation and you write to me again tothat effect I will
be glad to furnish it,

R.L.   Yours truly,

                              Can.Imm.Agt.

*Letter sent by Canadian Immigration Department to Ed Gifford, age 23,
in Boston who had requested information about homesteading in
Western Canada.*

on this particular day he had bad news for her: before going west,
he had been involved with an eastern Canadian girl who had
turned down his offer of marriage. Now she had written to say she
had changed her mind and they could be married after all. He
broke the sad news to Isabel as gently as he could. To no avail, she
was devastated. After two disappointments, this seemed the last,
cruel straw. She pleaded with him to not desert her and her pleas
were effective: Ed promised to write to his eastern friend and tell
her that he had found a true love in the west. And he did that, Ed

and Isabel were married, October 23, 1912, a date that has significance on our family calendar.

Isabel was a thrifty, dedicated housekeeper and wife. Babies made their appearance in predictable procession: Jean Elizabeth, July 2, 1914; Ina Beatrice, January 30, 1916; Lois Isabel, October 8, 1918; Eva Marjory, July 20, 1920; Edward James, April 3, 1922; John Elder, October 8, 1923.

As was common at that time, there were many miscarriages and stillborns. I recall being called into my mother's bedroom and asked if I wanted to "See the baby before it died." As I was at the age when little girls adore babies, that was a painful experience. I had previously helped my mother sort out the big box of baby clothes and was devastated when I tore the fragile lace on a little sleeve. Now, the loss of the baby made me cringe with guilt, if I had not torn the lace, this might not have happened. I don't know how or where or when the little premature body was disposed of; perhaps it was just as well we were not told.

They say a cook is either a good meat cook or a good pastry cook, but rarely both. My mother excelled in meat cooking: huge roasts of beef or pork from animals killed on the farm. Big whitefish were brought down from northern Saskatchewan lakes in the winter and kept frozen in an empty granary. I didn't like having to scale the fish. I did not have a knack for it, the large scales resisted and flew into my face no matter how hard I tried to avoid them, and I hated the smell. My mother cooked the fish with milk in a large shallow pan in the cookstove oven. I don't know what seasoning she might have used, but the thick, white flesh was absolutely delicious. One big fish made a tasty meal for the whole family.

After the beef carcass was solidly frozen, my father would bring in a quarter, place it on the cleared kitchen table, and then the work began. The children's job was to steady the slippery, fat-covered carcass that had a tendency to slide with each cut of the saw. My father had spent hours sharpening the blade for the occasion. He would clamp the saw into a vise in the kitchen and the piercing sound of the triangular rasp on metal was almost more than the human ear could endure. My father seemed to like sharpening cutting tools and he even did it for neighbours. The rest of his family certainly did not appreciate his endeavours.

I did not realize it at the time, but the dissection of the carcasses was a good education in beef and pork lore. We learned which were the choicest cuts; even to this day when I pass a meat counter, I know which part of the carcass a cut came from and why it may be preferred to others. After the beef, the pork was much easier to handle, possibly because it had more fat.

All the meat would be stored securely in the empty granary until the spring breakup. My mother canned whatever beef might be left. She would cut it in stew-size pieces, put it in glass sealers with a bit of water and salt and boil the sealers in the copper tub of water for hours. I cannot recall that she ever lost a jar through cracking or spoilage.

The pork was committed to a barrelful of brine in our earth cellar under the house. It cured well down there but it was an unpleasant task to bring up a pork roast; it could slither out of our hands and fall back into the barrel while we kept a watchful eye out for the lizards that were the denizens of our deep. Getting the eggs out of the waterglass crock was almost as bad: we groped around in the congealed mass to locate the eggs and then hoped to get them upstairs intact. My mother put the eggs down in waterglass for cooking and baking as the hens did not lay in the cold henhouse in winter. The first fresh egg in the spring was an event. My father always got the first egg and as children we would stand around watching in envy as he ate it. To this day, a fresh egg is something I never take for granted.

My mother made her own soap from the fat rendered from pork. She also made delicious headcheese from (guess what?) the pig's head. For the soap, she boiled up a concoction of fat and lye and poured it into a wood trough, partitioned in bar sizes, that my father had made. She used the home-made soap for the laundry. Occasionally, a 'boughten' cake of Fels Naptha would find its way into our orbit and, like the cake of Bon Ami used for cleaning the windows, it was considered a luxury. We bought our toilet soap, the red Lifebuoy and the green Palmolive.

When you consider that my mother knitted all of our long, black stockings, sweaters, mitts and scarves, "women's work is never done," certainly applied to her. She read while she knitted. By the standards of the day, she was considered to be well educated, having received her high school education in Scotland. To assuage her thirst for reading, she had the Provincial Government send their travelling libraries to our home regularly. What treasures they contained, such a variety of subjects and authors. I read voraciously.

In the winter, when my parents thought I was asleep, I would creep out to the livingroom and read by the light from the heater's glowing coals, which shone through the hard mica on the heater's large door. No wonder I needed glasses when I was eleven!

My mother also kept the post office; a rural post office called "Piche". As our district was almost a hundred percent anglo, mostly Scots, the name of the post office was certainly a misnomer. There is a story behind it. Apparently the Federal Post Master of the day had assured a good friend that he would name a post office after him: the Post Master was from Quebec, so that is how an anglophone community had a French name on their post office. I used to help my mother by wielding the cancellation device on the George V three cent stamps. The cancellation mark was an oval with bars, today a sought-after collector item.

The Piche post office served a wide community. The mail was brought out from Harris, sixteen miles away, by democrat in the summer and by sleigh in the winter. The mail carrier, Mr. Wilkinson, had a high-spirited team of carriage horses that brought him through good or bad roads and weather. The big hazard in the spring, apart from the muddy trails, was Eagle Creek which had a habit of overflowing its steep banks; occasionally it would be impossible to ford. My mother had a good rapport with Mr. Wilkinson and he would bring her emergency supplies from town though that was not part of his job, and would certainly be frowned upon by the postal authorities, who took their positions very seriously. Mr. Wilkinson did not look like a postman, he looked like a college professor . . . bookish. Perhaps that is why he and our mother were kindred spirits. So the people who came to our house took home both mail and books, and the memory of good conversation and congeniality. It made for a happy home.

If many children, a demanding husband, the post office and the library were not enough, my mother also boarded the school teacher. His name was George Lyon, a young man who had come to our district, by way of relatives, from Toronto. George and my father and mother made a congenial trio. In the evening they would play whist and five hundred by the hour, all the while Mr. Lyon would be keeping a sharp eye out for those of us wrestling with homework. We could never have a valid excuse for not doing our homework . . . Mr. Lyon knew all. Sometimes a neighbour who had dropped by for the mail, would join the card game. The house would be blue with smoke from hand-rolled cigarettes and my father's pipe; not one of us contracted lung cancer!

The trouble with life and our unending quest for happiness is that we usually do not know until much later, in retrospect, that the time through which we had just lived would be memorable. We all recognize catastrophe, disillusion and heartbreak when it is happening, but happiness is ephemeral, a bubble in the wind, and we do not recognize until it is long past, "That was a good time." The twenties were a good time for us, as they ideally should be for the four-to-fourteen-year-old decade of our lives. I had done well in school and was sent to Saskatoon to attend grade eleven when I was fourteen. My older sister, Jean, had gone to collegiate there a year before. We stayed in a residence ominously called The Presbyterian School Home for Girls. Today, that name would indicate that The Home harboured delinquents; discipline was as severe as if we were and the place as joyless. I did not fit in well. Fortunately, for me, my parents found they could not afford to keep both of us in the costly establishment (the crop had been a disaster), so Ina stayed home after Christmas and Jean finished her high school there; she had always been one grade ahead of me since she skipped grade two. We had started at our rural school together, the winter I had just turned five: the purpose in sending me was to keep Jean company, but then who in their right mind wants to be shut up with a rambunctious five-year-old in winter? . . . certainly not my pragmatic parents.

After the School Home sojourn, I continued my studies through a Government correspondence course at home. The ugly thirties were just settling in, the relentless winds were tearing Saskatchewan farm land asunder, The Stock Exchange crash was beginning to inflict its invidious aftermath that was felt around the world. My mother became pregnant; her youngest child, John, was seven and the end of her years of arduous child-raising should have been in sight. My parents rationalized the pregnancy by saying that this would be someone to look after them in their old age. Robbie Burns got it right when he said something about the best-laid plans of mice and men often going off the track!

We had a 1931 summer that was full of uncertainty. Once again, the lack of rain was responsible for a sub-average crop. I had completed the correspondence course, but what was next? Jean and I, particularly, lolled about disconsolately, both eager to get on with our lives. I did not feel any great anticipation about a new baby in the household. The summer wore on, hot, dreary and dry, the summer of our discontent.

The baby was due in October; our mother went down to Rosetown, 25 miles away, to await her confinement. She already had two October babies, both on October 8th, five years apart, but this baby was tardy in arriving. Finally, she had another girl (another girl!), Iris, nine pounds, six ounces on October 23rd, her parents nineteenth wedding anniversary. All went well, until Dr. George phoned to tell my father that our mother was running a fever. My father was alarmed. The children did not know it at the time, but my mother had had a dream in her late pregnancy, a vivid premonition that she would not survive. She had contracted the fever shortly before the end of the ten-day confinement; child-bed fever it was called and, before antibiotics, was often fatal.

My father led Jean and I into his bedroom and we held hands as we knelt by the bed and prayed. My father was buoyed with hope when they phoned from the hospital the next day to say that she was a little better. But the next day word was sent that perhaps one of the family should come down to be with her. I was sent. We never spoke to each other, she was delirious when I got there. I sat by her bedside and attempted to feed her the corn soup the hospital provided, but she did not respond. All she did was repeat the names of her children, over and over: Jean, Ina, Lois, Eva, Edward, John. My father asked me after if she had called out his name, she had not, but of course I lied to spare him more grief. My mother died at 5 a.m. November 11th, 1931. Iris was nineteen days old. It was a cold, bleak day, Friday, November 13th when the funeral was held from our home that overflowed with mourners. Our mother's open casket was in the living room; she was wearing her only good dress, the brown one that I did not like. Our father, with his children grouped around him, sat near the casket. He said later that a strange thing happened, his overpowering grief was, for a few moments, replaced by overpowering joy as though his beloved 'Tot' was telling him that she had gone to joyful repose.

After the service, the funeral cortege wended its slow way from our farm, by the barn, down the familiar hilly roads, past Hillview school (flag at half mast), and finally, to the Harris cemetery. Burial was in the Elder plot, where both of my mother's parents had been interred the year before, and before that, her sister Bessie, in 1923.

It is now the final resting place of all seven Elders, who came as a family unit from Scotland.

End of an era; I left feeling both cross and sad. With the captain gone from our ship, my brothers and sisters and I set sail on the rough sea of maturement. It was a rough journey. Our father pretty well abandoned ship, certainly none of his crew of seven, ranging in age from seventeen to infant, could rely on him to guide us safely into port. For that reason, we became strongly individualistic; we had lost our common point of reference, the tie that bound us together. Contrary to what might be expected, we did not form strong bonds with each other, those bonds came much later in our lives.

Jean, who in maturity changed her name to Bethal Phaigh, left home when she turned eighteen in 1932. She went to Saskatoon, married, and raised one son, David Graham. After her husband, Gordon, died in 1964, age 50, she abandoned her profitable Regina business, designing and crafting crests, and set out to 'find herself'; this quest took her to university in British Columbia and from there to San Francisco at the height of the Haight/Ashbury era.

Her involvement in the mores of the day led her from gestalt with Fritz Perl to Japanese reiki with its 'hands-on healing' message. She built herself a cabin on a mountain in the Nelson, B.C. area where she counselled groups who came to her from all over the world. Her winters were spent with similar groups in Hawaii. At a gathering of our family in Saskatoon, June, 1980, she remarked to our daughter-in-law who was seated beside her, "I don't belong among these people." She was right... she never did 'belong.'

Jean died of cancer January 3, 1986; she had followed the injunctions of an old Doukhobor woman, but the home cure did not work. As she lay dying in a Richmond, B.C. hospital, she requested that a friend with her ask the nurses to have no lights in her room. The nurses complied; the friend left the dark room for a few minutes; when she returned she found that the room was brightly lit. The friend went to the nurses' station to complain, the nurse's reply was: "There were no lights on in that room." Jean had just died. She had gone out in a blaze of glory.

As for me, age 15 when our mother died, I fell into the tentacles of 'retail' after I left home at nineteen. Retail involved me in advertising, a course I pursued through many ups and downs. There was marriage at twenty-six to handsome and popular Henry Van Dyck.

A son, Clayton and twin daughters, Carol and Karen, followed in rapid succession. Our tall, svelte daughters ended up in Toronto for a short career as models, then marriage.

Our son, after getting his first degree from university when he was twenty, spent time in Ghana as a teacher, near Tarkwa. Then it was back to Canada and two more degrees. He continues to make Saskatoon his home, though his work with a large pharmaceutical firm gives him many frequent flier points; technological linkage makes his choice of domicile feasible. Three times married, no children.

Lois, who I abandoned to her stint of caring for the family when she was sixteen, took a course in hairdressing in Saskatoon when it came her turn to leave. She married Jim Proudfoot in December, 1939, when she was twenty one. Jim was in the Canadian army until the end of the war, when they moved to Vancouver with their two young daughters, Marilyn and Joan. Lois and Jim still live in the home they bought in Richmond, B.C. in 1956. Lois was the secure, sensible, motherly one, a superb homemaker, the one we could all count upon for loving advice and support. The world, for us, would have been a much darker place without Lois.

Eva, who was eleven when our mother died, was full of energy, gregarious, clever. Her choice of vocation was a business course in Saskatoon after she left the farm when our father sold it; she was then eighteen. She boarded with me, in the lovely home of Henrietta and Tom Fraser on Bedford Road in Saskatoon. She enlisted in the navy, not in the clerical field in which she was trained, but as an officers' cook, a field that took her from Halifax to Victoria (where she baked tea biscuits for Lord and Lady Athlone). Her nickname was 'Petey' and she was always fun to be around. After the war, she married Earl Lunde in Calgary, had two children, Glenna and Robert, and lived in Richmond, B.C. (near Lois) until her affliction, multiple sclerosis, ended her life when she was fifty-three. An assessment of her spirit can be summarized in the fact that, when she was crippled with M.S. her United Church visitation group took her with them to visit others who were not ambulant so she could cheer them up. That was Petey!

The boys probably suffered most from the loss of their mother. Ted, who was nine, missed her most of all, she had always been the champion of his causes. In a family of achieving students, he was not an achiever, he hated school. Mr. Lyon, the teacher, made no

apology for his dislike of Ted. In hindsight, I think that Ted may
have suffered from a learning dysfunction, which, in a rural school
at that time, would not even be considered. Ted was in school when
I left home; he was sixteen when our father packed it in on the farm
in 1938. Ted may not have excelled at school, but he was a natural
mechanic, a talent that stood him in good stead when he joined the
Air Force in that capacity. Air force training was his apprenticeship
where he learned the skills of restoration. After the war, he used
that skill to restore an old car, a rare Corde that had been found
in a Saskatchewan farmer's yard by a Saskatoon business man. I have
a newspaper clipping lauding Ted's work. Ted married, had three
children, then divorced. He gravitated to the Yukon where he died
from a gunshot wound (murder or suicide?), before he was fifty.
Ted was someone who was born out of his time, he belonged to
the frontier days. He is buried in the old timers' section of the cemetery in Whitehorse, Yukon. Had our mother lived, it is interesting
to speculate what direction Ted's life might have taken. He was tall,
rugged, handsome, cast in the adventurer's mould.

I always feel bad when I think of my brother, John, who had just
turned eight when our mother died. He never had a Christmas gift
after he was seven, our father did not believe in Christmas. It would
not have made much difference even if he had been a Christmas
enthusiast, there was simply no money for such folly. I don't know
why it bothers me that John was deprived of Christmas when he
was so young, the rest of us were deprived of it, too. John was what
Ted was not, a serious student. When he left the farm and went to
Saskatoon, he was almost fifteen. He fell into the clutches of a
large, lovely boarding house, most were university students. John
worked for his board and room there while he continued high
school. The landlady was a mean taskmaster: when John looked
forward to visiting the Saskatoon Exhibition, which he had never
seen, she told him he could not go because he had not achieved
the desired shine on her hardwood floors. He stayed there, however, until he had nearly completed grade twelve when he went to
Brandon to join the Royal Canadian Air Force. He was nineteen
when he was commissioned a Pilot Officer. He saw duty overseas
(visited Iris in Scotland), and at the end of the war he returned
to Saskatoon to finish grade twelve and get a degree in account-
ing from the University. He married well, the daughter of an ex-
mayor, they had three sons, John, Tom and Gordon. My brother

John rejoined the Air Force as an Accounts Officer and spent years in Europe, his extracurricular interest there being art; when the family returned to Canada, they had many beautiful paintings for their big home in Ottawa. John's full name is John Elder Gifford: he has lived up to the fine Elder heritage.

Iris was seven when our father determined that she would go to Scotland to live with our mother's sister, Agnes, who had remained in Scotland when her parents emigrated. Iris made the journey to Scotland, unaccompanied, in the Spring of 1939. A name tag was pinned to her clothes, and a kind couple, taking the same train kept an eye on her. On the ship across the Atlantic, she was coddled by passengers who felt sorry for the little, lone traveller. Aunt Agnes and her husband had arranged to go out to the vessel before it docked: when Iris was lowered to the dory, panic set in, there she was, without a friend, in a strange land, in the hands of strangers who spoke a strange language; she cried hysterically. Aunt Agnes had made a wise decision: she and her husband, with their son, Hugh, took Iris on a vacation in the Highlands as an introduction to her new life. I am ashamed to say that we did not keep in touch with Iris as we should have. Aunt Agnes had requested, through our father, that we not communicate with our little sister as she wanted the bonds broken. It was sad that we obeyed her injunction. I will always cherish the memory of my last evening with Iris before she left for Scotland. Charlie Allen and I took her for a ride, she sat on the front seat between us. When she and I were alone for a few minutes, she looked up at me very seriously and said, "I'm going to miss all my sisters, especially you, Ina." I did not see her again until 1967, when, with my daughter, Karen, we visited Iris's home near Lanark. I was the first of the family to do so, though all of her siblings, except Ted, finally did – many several times. My father had made the journey to Scotland in 1950, before Iris and Peter Horsborough were married. They have three daughters, Fay, Anne and Lynn and many grandchildren. Iris enjoys travelling and has visited Canada often, she prefers B.C. to the prairies and Toronto! Four of our mother's children are still alive: John in Ottawa, Lois in Vancouver, Iris in Scotland and me, Ina, in Toronto. The inevitable afflictions of old age are upon us and we shall endure them with good grace and equanimity, as we should; we learned early how to endure.

The Light Blue Dress

The Eaton's catalogue, as in most farm families when I was growing up, was our shopping mall. I don't think my mother ever
entered a ready-to-wear store after she was married and she certainly didn't buy much for herself, even from the catalogue.

After the harvest was in, huge parcels, veritable cornucopias of
winter wear would come by mail, but they contained no dress for
our mother. She bought hers from the sale catalogues or clearance
sheets where you provided sketchy choices: colour, preferred material, size. Then you took your chance, but you knew with the con-
fidence of a died-in-the-wool Eaton customer that money would be
cheerfully refunded if the goods were not satisfactory.

I recall, for special reasons, two of the dresses my mother got
by the 'chancey' route. The first was one I loved, a light blue crepe,
a very impractical dress for a farmer's wife far removed from a dry
cleaners. She tried it on, of course, as soon as it came in the mail
and then it was put aside in its box, kept for a special occasion.
That occasion soon arose, a farewell evening for a neighbour;
everyone would be there.

She had her dress; she would have to do something about her
hair. When she was younger, in the style of the time, my mother
had worn her hair in a bun at the top of her head. When she put
on her Queen Mary-style hat with the feathers, she would use a
long, ornate hatpin to anchor the hat to the bun. I didn't like
watching as I was sure the hatpin went right through her skull. In
the 20's when women raised their hemlines, danced the charleston,
took up smoking, they even bobbed their long hair! Our mother
was the first in our staid district to do so, bob her hair that is.

Before getting dressed for the big farewell event, she marcelled
her hair. The marcel iron was metal, two pieces that clamped
together over the hair with undulations that created the wave. The
right heat was vital; the heat source was the cookstove and the right-
ness of the heat was determined by a wet finger. It was a delicate
operation but when it was done our mother's thin, straight hair
had achieved a whole new dimension. It looked lovely!

As she pulled the new blue dress over her newly marcelled hair, we young ones watched in admiration. The crepe material was so soft, the colour just right, the fine clean line of the dress suited her. The belt, with its sparkling rhinestone buckle would provide the finishing touch; it was the prettiest thing we had ever seen, that buckle.

She was in a bit of a hurry as she smoothed the dress over her hips and told us to hand her the belt. But where was it? Didn't anyone know? Frantically, we all searched for it, every place it might be and every place it might not. It could not be found.

Now it was time to go, the rig was at the door; she flung a cardigan sweater over the pretty blue dress to disguise the fact that the belt was missing and, good sport that she was, she went and had a very good time. My father rarely went... he was not a good-time person.

The riddle of the missing belt was solved the next morning when the cold ashes of the cookstove were shaken down; they yielded up their treasure, the rhinestone buckle, its sparkle now dulled. The belt had been concealed in the tissue paper in the cardboard dress box which had helped provide the heat for the marcelling of hair.

Oh yes, about the second dress, another catalogue special years later. I never liked it, it was brown with an ecru lace modesty filling the V-neck. Brown was not her colour. In retrospect, I like it even less – it was the dress in which she was buried.

Homework

In the dictionary the word mangle has two distinctly different meanings: in the first listing it is 'something that spoils, ruins, or spoils badly.' In the second listing it is a 'machine for smoothing or pressing cloth.' In my home we did not have a pressing mangle, but my grandmother Elder did. It was kept outside the house in an adjoining working shed and, like everything used in domestic work when I was young, it was operated by hand, to press tablecloths, pillowcases, even sheets. We had not yet entered the convenience of the electrical age.

When my mother did the family wash each week, she used soap that she had made from animal fat and lye. Occasionally, she would indulge in a 'boughten' cake of Fels Naptha, or some other cake of laundry soap . . . no flakes. I recall one illustration on a laundry soap wrapper because it was so incongruous! it showed a beautifully dressed and coiffed matron seated at a piano enjoying her leisure. In our household there was no leisure on washday. The wash water had been readied the day before and, depending on the season, it would be melted snow or ice, a barrelful from the slough, or one from the well, softened with lye. The kitchen stove would be lit early in the morning, the big copper boiler that covered the two stove lids, filled with water, the cake of soap sliced thinly into the water which would be brought to a boil. The 'white wash' was always boiled on the stove and was the first into the washing machine.

The wooden washing machine had been carried in from the shed adjoining the house. The four legged washing machine was round, with a hinged wooden lid. Four wooden pegs that swirled the clothes in the water were inside, with the operating gears on the lid outside. Guess who operated the long handle that activated the washing mechanism? When they were available, it would be child power and when they were in school, it was mother power. As a last resort, especially in winter, it was father power, but that did not happen often. We always had large washes, the teacher's white shirts had priority. Water was kept hot on top of the stove and the loads succeeded each other in order of darkness. My father's work clothes were usually last in the machine. It was an all day job.

It was not just the physically tiring operation of the machine, twenty minutes to each load, and the equally tiring hand-turned wringer, but the heavy loads had to be carried to the outdoor clothes line which was propped up half way down with a long stick. Even when it was freezing outside, my mother would hang clothes on the line as they smelled better, and seemed whiter, than when they were dried on the many lines strung the length of the kitchen. There was one hazard to freezing clothes outside when we carried them in stiff as a board there was a danger that, if they were allowed to bend, they would break, especially the men's long woolen underwear. I had one bad experience washing wool after my mother died. I put the baby's clothes in the boiler on the stove and when it was time to remove them, the little wool shirt was in shreds. No one had told me you could not boil wool!

The difference between laundry day at our house and at Grandma's was the difference between night and day. Grandma Elder had an engine to operate her machine. Setting up the washing machine was Uncle Jim's job. He had a half horsepower motor (now in a museum) that he set up outside the kitchen door and connected to the washing machine in the kitchen with a long belt. The sound of that little motor seemed deafening, but it did its job well. There was no laborious hand-pumping on the Elders' washday and they might even have had time to sit down to their piano, but that would have been unheard of in the middle of a weekday in a stern Scot household!

Monday was washday, on Tuesday we ironed. The flatirons, as they were called, were heavy metal with wide, polished surfaces. They had a bar in the top centre, to which the handle could be attached. The handle had a locking device and a wooden hand grip. It was a wrist-breaker. The big hazard when ironing was to keep the top of the cookstove clean. If a stove lid had to be lifted to replenish wood or coal, there was always the danger that a speck of ash would end up as a black smudge on a shirt collar that had been given such meticulous care in the white wash. So ironing was something of a delicate operation, and tiring. The materials in garments and household articles were mostly cotton or linen. Neither was easy to iron; everything had to be sprinkled, rolled up tightly so the dampness would be uniform and ironed while it was still damp. There were no synthetics to make linen or cotton more crease resistant, so the effort put into removing all wrinkles by ironing would soon be counteracted in the first wearing. Wrinkles were considered the mark of a poor housekeeper; for housekeepers it was a losing battle! Rayon, produced from wood fibre, was introduced as an alternative, but it too wrinkled easily and was not a desirable alternative to cotton and linen except that it was cheaper and lighter in weight, The quality of the 'good' cotton when I was a child was superlative: Egyptian cotton was especially fine, and we took it for granted.

When woolens were ironed with the old flatirons, a pressing cloth would be dampened, placed directly on the garment, and the hot iron applied. A cloud of steam that could have been scalding was the result. George Lyon, the teacher, would press his own pants, but by this time we had a new gas iron that had to be pumped. Not long ago, I was in an antique shop when an old gas iron was brought in; the same vintage as the one Mr. Lyon used to get the perfect press on his garments. It made me nostalgic to see it. I'm sure antique dealers are tired of hearing, "My grandmother had one just like that": I almost said, "Oh, we had an iron just like that," but I didn't. We did not have the luxury of a folding ironing board; it was either a wide board on the dining room table, or in the summer, near the kitchen stove, laid across the wide arms of my father's oak chair. Ironing was a tolerable chore in the cool weather, but in the heat of summer, it was almost unbearable. Knowing housewives did their ironing at the same time as they baked bread in the summer... get it all over with at once. The heat of the iron was determined by a wet finger on the flat surface (the saliva test!).

Bread baking was a never-ending job when there were so many mouths to feed. The big blue enamelled breadpan was a fixture in almost every home. It had to be big to accommodate the dough required for the large loaves that would fill the oven to capacity. When I was twelve, my mother was away for a few days and we were running out of bread. My father tongue-lashed me because I did not know how to bake bread. It was a skill I had to master after our mother died. I had many trial-and-error efforts. The yeast was in cakes that had to be dissolved in lukewarm water. Temperatures were vital, the right temperature for the yeast, the right temperature in the room for the dough to rise and, finally, the right temperature for the loaves to rise again after they had been shaped and put in the individual pans. Finally, the baking temperature had to be maintained evenly in the cookstove. The sound as you tapped the bottom of the baked loaf would indicate if it was done. Keeping the right temperature was not easy in a stove that was fuelled by dried cow pancakes from the pasture, one of our main sources of fuel during the depression years.

One rainy summer day after my mother had died and my father was away somewhere, I kneaded the dough in the big pan, put on the lid and set the pan on top of the warming oven on the cookstove. Then I remembered that my father had told me to keep an eye on the cow in the pasture as she was due to freshen. As the day was rainy and chilly, I thought I should run down to the pasture to check on her. She was not in sight so I hurried down to the far end of the pasture where she was likely to be if she was calving. Sure enough, she had had her calf and the poor little thing was not on its feet as it should have been. I knew I would have to act fast so I ran the half mile up to the barn, hitched a horse to the stoneboat and drove down to the pasture to rescue the wee animal. The cow did not take kindly to my efforts to save her calf. I finally got it on the stoneboat and she followed me anxiously as I took the two to the safety and comfort of the barn. By the time I had them bedded down and the horse watered and fed, I had been gone much longer than I anticipated when I had left the house.

As I entered the kitchen, an amazing sight greeted me. The dough in the bread pan had risen, and risen, like a monstrous white mushroom. It had lifted the big lid and was about to come crashing down on all sides. Whew, just in time, I punched it down, shaped the loaves, and kept my fingers crossed that the yeast had not expended all of its risibility in that one big effort. The miracle was that it had performed so well in a cold kitchen and then managed to rise in loaf form so well again. After that, I knew I knew how to bake bread. As for the calf, it survived and thrived.

Everything we did on the farm seemed to require much physical effort. Machinery, such as the fanning mill used to separate chaff from the seed grain, had to be turned by hand. The big heavy meat grinder was hand operated, as were the churn and the washing machine. We got down on our knees to scrub the wooden kitchen floor that forever seemed to need cleaning. The first congoleum had been laid in the living room. Eventually, it was replaced and relaid in the kitchen. Up until then, my mother had scrubbed that wood on the kitchen floor, on her knees, for years. All the while, my father bought nothing but the best in tools for his workshop. It was a man's world when I was young!

It was a matter of pride to keep the top of the cookstove black, using blackener. It was best to apply the liquid when the stove was barely warm. After it dried, the top had to be rubbed and polished, a dirty chore. I wonder now why we bothered as even one drop of our hard well water spilled on the stove, turned white. It was a thankless task.

The sides of the stove and the winter-heater fared better. It was one of the penalties we paid for having people in and out of our house to use the post office and the library. We had to maintain a reasonably high standard of housekeeping. Tuesday and Friday were mail days, the days of the heaviest traffic, and work!

Our house had started out as a homesteader's wooden shack. The shack metamorphosed into a living room as the family expanded, and the house with it. Two bedrooms were added on the north and the big kitchen on the south. The kitchen had an innovation, for that time, a separate cupboard section. There was a large flour bin that held at least a hundred pounds of flour in the centre of the counter, with shelves and cupboards above and below. My mother used the cover of the flour bin section, turned over, as the board on which to roll cookies and pies.

It was neat and handy. At the far end of the cupboard area there was a jog that housed the cream separator and, above that, the post office boxes for the dozen or so families who came to the Piche Post Office. My mother would use the flat cupboard top as her desk as she did the required paper work for the post office. I loved that cosy corner; it was my mother's retreat and work place whether she was cutting the meat from a pig's head for head cheese, or perusing the Eaton catalogue without child-distraction. I liked to help in the post office by cancelling the three cent stamps, the definitives of the day, by using the barred cancellation stamper, a collector's item now. The big, grey box that contained the Traveling Library from Regina, stood under the small window at the end of the cupboard area. How I would like to have a list of the magical contents of any of those library boxes today!

The kitchen had a big, wooden table which held a large water crock as well as a pail of well water. The five gallon can of coal oil for the lamps was in the corner behind the door. A cabinet held a wash basin, water jug and had a rail for the face towels. The original living room had sensible brown burlap half way up the walls; the top half and the ceiling were papered. There was no such thing as prepasted wallpaper so the application of the paper with its thick hand-applied glue, was a challenge to patience and endurance. It would be done when the children were in school. I liked the pattern of the brown-toned paper on the walls above the burlap. As all farm houses were furnished with basic necessities, there was not much variety. I recall thumbing through an Eaton sale furniture catalogue when I was about twelve and being dismayed with the realization that, if I ever had to furnish a home, I would have no idea what to choose. My interest in home furnishings came to fruition years later when I was employed by a major chain of fine furniture retailers and, as part of my duties, I was required to have a thorough knowledge of every facet of the furniture business, from advertising to buying, even designing! My inhibitions were laid to rest.

There was little luxury china and few ornaments in our home, but my mother had a perfume bottle I coveted. It had been given to her by Mr. Ogle, the Raleigh man, who had stabled his horse and stayed at our home overnight. The 'Raleigh Man' and the 'Watkins Man' each included our home on their rounds, perhaps twice a year. They carried in their rigs merchandise that we bought regularly... a special Raleigh's Ointment that was used on the horses' shoulders when the collar rubbed them raw. My father bought small bottles of a potent medicine, 'Dr. Bells' that he swore by for the animals, and was even known to coerce a few drops into an ailing child! My mother replenished her tins of baking powder and spices from the itinerant merchants, believing that the quality was superior to that of the brands available in the town stores. As children, we all loved it when the Raleigh or Watkins man came.

The bottle of perfume was frosted glass with a matching stopper. To me it represented the ultimate in luxury, and I still have a special liking for frosted glass. I wish I had that bottle that stood on my mother's dresser long after the perfume was used and the scent was gone.

In the warm weather, a farmyard with animals never lacked flies. My grandfather Elder used to recite a little verse that went like this:

Big fleas have little fleas
Upon their backs to bite them,
Little fleas have lesser fleas
and so ad infinitum!

Strangely, I do not recall our dogs ever having fleas, but, in summer, they could harbour a wood tick or two on their necks. Father would remove the ugly tick with pliers, but there was always the danger of leaving the sucking head intact in the animal. It was more efficient to apply a lighted match to the tick's body and it would then immediately relinquish its hold. There was a downside, the hazard of setting fire to the dog!

The horses had the voraciously biting horse flies to plague them, though I'm not sure which were worse, the big horse flies or the invisible nose flies. When the horses went out to work, nose bags that kept the nose flies at bay were a must. In the pasture, the horses would patrol the pasture fence, swinging their heads up and down, up and down, trying to evade the tormenting nose flies.

Our house had well-secured screen windows, but house flies were not easily deterred. The blue bottles and others would cling to the screen on the kitchen door, daring anyone to open it long enough for them to enter. They were particularly numerous when a storm was brewing. A screen door black with clinging flies was the harbinger of a storm.

We swatted and swatted flies on our white kitchen walls, where they naturally left their mark. We hung sticky, spiral hangers from the ceilings; the flies would become impaled, buzzing frantically while they tried to get free. "Don't get your hair caught!" We filled old pie plates with brown pads (of I don't know what), added a bit of water, and that brew took care of a few. There were usually one or two of those pie-plate-type fly traps on the platform at the front of our school room. "Don't step in it."

Fall was the worst time for flies in the house, their instinct was to try to escape winter by spending it inside in warmth. That's when the fly sprayer came into full play. It was a tin sprayer with an attached container that would be filled with a liquid called Flit. We pumped and pumped that sprayer until our arms ached; no aerosol in those days, it was all manual. But there was really no relief from the house flies until the blessed first frost. The odd fly would remain in the house sometimes, to become almost a pet. It was a reminder that winter had its upside as well as its down . . . no more fly invasions!

There was always lots of smoke in our house what with the men smoking pipes and cigarettes, the smoke from the coal and wood burned in the cookstove and winter heater, not to mention the grease smoke from the generous use of fat in the frying pan and the big pot of it for the golden doughnuts that were our delight on a cold winter's night. The doughnut fat was recycled to end up as soap (with the help of the right proportion of lye) . . . more smoke! Yes, there was lots of smoke.

Our father's pipe had a stem that curved down toward his chest, the big, heavy bowl generated plenty of smoke and had to be reamed out regularly to keep it in top functioning condition. The teacher's pipe was more elegant with straight stem and bowl. One neighbour's contribution to the smokey atmosphere was a corn-cob pipe that was as efficient at smoke production as its more refined companions. There were clay pipes in our house too, but the only use for them was the blowing of bubbles from the soapy water prepared by our mother. We liked to put the bowl of the clay pipe just below the surface and see how much foam we could generate.

All of that smoke in confined quarters settled on the painted walls of the kitchen and on the living room wallpaper. There was only one way to clean it off: soap and water for the kitchen and flour and water dough for the wallpaper. It took just the right mix of flour and water to form the dough that could be rolled in large balls across the paper and not stick to it. It was very efficient at removing the sooty grime from the paper. It was also fun, at first, but young arms soon tired and interest waned. Every household had its favourite blend of flour and water with a little bit of something added to increase efficiency; salt and washing soda were two favourites but, just like the ads for household cleaners a couple of generations later, the proficiency was sometimes exaggerated. But one thing was sure, whatever was used, the smoke settled over the surface again . . . woman's work was never done! And the men had the pleasure of generating much of it; smoking was almost totally a male indulgence.

I recall, as a child, marvelling at the extent of my father's addiction to tobacco, both chewing and smoking. The Ogden's Cut Plug he chewed was reserved mostly for the field, and I can understand how its use would modify the dry dust from the land he was tilling. For the cigarettes and pipe, he bought large tins of fine cut and rolled his cigarettes by hand until, later, a device for home-rolling cigarettes came on the scene; that was a large step forward.

But to get back to the day I realized he was an addict, we were riding together on the spring seat of the big sleigh box. It was cold, cold as a Saskatchewan winter combined with wind can be. My father wore big leather gauntlets, lined with wool, on his hands as the weary horses plodded home through heavy snow. He removed the gauntlets, handed the reins to me, got his tobacco pouch out of a pocket of his big buffalo skin coat and attempted to roll a cigarette . . . it was not a complete success. He tried hard, however, to light it, striking wood match after match while protecting the feeble flame with his bare hands. He finally succeeded and I watched as he took deep, satisfying puffs. But, as he attempted to put his bare hands back into the gauntlets, a blast of wind whipped the cigarette from his mouth. He cursed but did not try to roll or light another, which seemed sensible to me; it was certainly not sensible to go to all that bother just to have a smoke!

But I cannot leave the subject of smoke without telling about the day we returned from school to find our mother finishing washing the large kitchen ceiling. My, it looked clean; there was still a small square to do and I shouted up to her on the ladder, "Why don't you leave that dirty piece so everybody can see how it used to look?" She did not heed my suggestion, but it was probably the closest she would get in the way of appreciation for her labour.

The stove pipes that snaked their way from the cookstove and the living room heater to the brick chimney in the kitchen were cleaned once a year, before the winter heater was removed and its pipes stored for the summer. The sections of the pipes would be taken down, placed on end outside and then gently tapped until the soot fell out. It was a dirty job and certainly not one to be done on a windy day, but it was essential: sooty pipes caught fire, or in the winter, if ice and snow blocked the outside chimney vent, the fumes could (and have been known to), kill families as they slept. My father knew the cleanest burning coal; Drumheller anthracite was his choice, monster lumps of shiny black that had to be broken up with the back of an axe. There was very little slag in fine Drumheller coal. When your lives depend on something you soon learn to respect the very best.

Our house was always banked with dirt around the outside for winter, storm windows replaced the screens, and the summer screen door was replaced with a heavy wood door. Cold winters were anticipated and usually materialized, sometimes well before Christmas. With the house air-tight, stoves burning, men smoking, many children breathing, the oxygen in the house soon depleted. You could tell when it was getting low, children got drowsy, the light from the oil lamps dimmed . . . time to let in some air. A child would be sent to open the outside door, regardless of the cold outside. As soon as the door was opened, a great white cloud of steam rolled into the house dispelling torpor, a cold, refreshing cloud of the purest air in the world . . . prairie air.

 School

As with most children, school was a large part of our lives. The rural school we attended, built in 1912, was called Ailsa Craig (after the island in Scotland whose granite is used for the world's best curling stones!). There was no granite around our school, nor curling, just vast expanses of rich soil. The one-room wooden school, painted white, faced west with rows of windows north and south. The blackboard, (which was black!), reached across the east wall. This meant that almost all of the pupils who attended that school had to wear glasses before they reached adulthood. The light from the windows caused a glare on the blackboard which made it almost impossible to see anything on it for part of the day. No effort was made to correct the defect.

The single entrance to the school faced the main road on the west; there were two cloakrooms, boys' and girls' to the right and the left of the entrance. A big heater sat in the back left corner of the classroom; it was surrounded by a metal protector that supposedly made the circulation of the heat more uniform. The teacher stoked the stove with coal as required. Of course the children seated close to the stove were blessed or cursed depending on their heat/cold tolerance ... uniform heating it was not.

The parallel rows of desks, double for the juniors and single for the seniors, had folding slanted wood tops and seats and ornate black cast iron grillwork at the sides and legs. That ornate grillwork has special significance for me. I am repelled by the memory of my younger sister, Eva, having her hands tied down to the grillwork on each side of her desk. Her teacher said her constant movement made the students nervous. Eva was afflicted with what was then called St. Vitus Dance, which was probably a harbinger of the multiple sclerosis that would cause her death at age 53. It was a cruel thing for the teacher to do; I don't like to think about it.

Every desk had an inkwell, ballpoints were yet to come. The folding wood tops covered the storage space for books and scribblers. Pencils were supplied by the school but the pencil boxes were one item where individuality could be exercised. The Cadillac of wooden pencil boxes was the three-tiered model. Two sections above the base section swung away to provide storage for even the most ambitious pen and pencil collection. The removable metal nibs of the pens gave the user a choice of broad stroke to fine. The ink of choice was Waterman, dark blue, for use in the desk ink-well unless the student was affluent enough to own her own bottle of ink.

Textbooks were provided by the school. There were two history textbooks for the higher grades, the green book, a thick one, was Canadian history and the smaller, red, was British history. History was a serious subject. We had a thin book called Civics; I don't remember being very keen on civics. Like most young female students of the day, math was not high on my preferred list but I was acceptably proficient in it anyway, probably because my teacher from grades five to ten, George Lyon, was serious about math. On Friday we would have a group math session: the teacher would give a lengthy oral equation, and we had better be listening!

Another lesson I enjoyed was Geography. A large map of the world would be pulled down like a huge window blind; Mr. Lyon with his pointer would indicate a place on the globe and woe to those who did not know the name of the designated spot, be it isthmus, bay, city, country or sea. It was an exciting way to learn about the world. The big companion map of Canada received the same treatment. The Canadian map deviated from today's. The province of Manitoba, which was shown in red, was a mere square bordering on the U.S.A. Its boundary on that map did not extend to Hudson Bay.

Winter noon hours, when it was not too cold to go outside, were fun. The boys dug forts by excavating into the big, solid snow banks in the school yard. There would be a tunnel by which one entered the fort on hands and knees, a password would be required and altogether it was exciting and challenging, a great way to spend a lunch hour.

In the summer, we played football, boys against the girls. As the girls in our school vastly outnumbered the boys, the game was about even. I still bear the effect of one game where I was playing goalkeeper. The ball was close to the goal. As I took a big kick to knock it away, Bill Longworth kicked at the same moment to try and knock it in. He missed the ball and hit the inside of my right leg with his heavy work boot. I complained to my mother about my sore leg and when she got around to looking at it in a couple of days, the leg was black and blue from the knee to the ankle. There was no emergency department to visit, but why go anyway? I could walk and no skin was broken. Ever since, the bone in my right leg has been rough-textured in the part that took the kick, and I have always been fearful that Bill's boot might some day come back to haunt me.

I only attended the 1912 school for seven years because in 1928 it burned down. Word came by long distance call, a prolonged ring on the telephone that would alert the whole circuit, that the school house was burning. There was snow on the ground as Jean and I went with our father and George Lyon to witness the spectacle. It was in full blaze when we got there, a sight to behold. I was sad to see it go; it was my own school and I took a proprietary interest in it. Mr. Lyon was especially sad because his private books and papers were lost with it. A few days later, we children walked to the burned-out school and examined its entrails. All I found was the husk of a paintbox; from its location, I was sure it was mine.

We used an empty old farmhouse as our school while a bright, shiny new one with, wonder of wonders, a real cement basement, was erected. It never quite had as much character as the old one, but at least in the new school we could see the blackboard all day. The windows were on the west side. The unwieldy old stove was replaced by a furnace in the basement which was more discriminating about the evenness of its heat. There were inside (septic tank) toilets off each cloakroom, a luxury, especially in winter. But the basic elements, the teaching and discipline, remained the same. George Lyon was famed throughout the countryside for his school discipline. The strap was a reality then and he did not hesitate to use it as required. He had the natural disciplinary instincts of stern teachers.

This was graphically displayed one winter day when two visitors came to the new school. It was a rare event for anyone to come to the school and enter it during school hours. The discipline was such that, when they came into the classroom from the back, not one child's head turned to see who the visitors were. I didn't think anything of it at the time, but later in life I marvelled at Mr. Lyon's ability to run a tight ship!

The school Christmas concert, a thing of sweat and splendour, played to a packed house. The quality of the Christmas concert was the bench mark for the quality of teaching and no effort was spared to put on a good show. Ours was usually one of the best, but the accolades should be reserved for the auxilliary help (mothers) who made the costumes to specifications, to the music teacher pressed into service from talent in the community, and to the general cooperation of the school board who were responsible for obtaining the floor-to-ceiling Christmas tree and the bags of candy for each and every child. I suppose it could be called the highlight of our school year.

Mr. Lyon was not a great teacher of art, but on a warm Friday afternoon in Spring, a child would be sent to find just the right crocus for an art lesson. Nature always provided a crocus in full bloom, a perfect speciman, newly released from its velvet-like cocoon which had protected it from the vagaries of Saskatchewan's weather.

The end of the year exams, in June, were taken seriously, very seriously. If even one subject was failed, the whole year had to be taken over again. Grades one to ten inclusive were taught in our rural school; there was no such frill as kindergarden. We had to go into the town of Harris to write our high school exams. Exams were an ordeal at best, but to have to go to a strange place to write them was intimidation at its most severe. The boys were more fortunate than the girls because they usually left school after grade eight or after they became fifteen, whichever came first. Their strong arms were required on the farm, education took a seat far back from the pragmatic necessity of working the land. Our father took a dim view of educating girls (who would only get married anyway, and thus have no need of an education!). But our mother was adamant that her girls would receive an advanced education. Advanced meant grades eleven and twelve, and those grades could only be obtained in the town or city. That dream died with her.

Mr. Lyon awarded prizes for excelling. One prize I received was a beautiful black Parker fountain pen with a gold-coloured lever that was used to pump the ink into a rubber tube in the pen barrel. The pen had a narrow black grosgrain ribbon so the proud owner could wear the pen around her neck. I put my new pen on proudly to wear home to show my mother. My father intercepted me before I got into the house and said I was to ride Jerry, the grey horse, to find the cows. They had been allowed to roam free as the crops were all harvested. Looking for the cows was no fun. True enough, Bessie, the big, red cow wore a bell, but she had mastered the art of even running without making it ring. I had asked my father to please put the bell on another cow, but he didn't.

Eventually Jerry and I found the cows, deep in a coulee, and herded them home, Jerry being as reluctant about the task as I was. Finally, I got home, bursting with eagerness to tell my mother about the wonderful fountain pen. I took my coat off to show her, but the only thing she could see was the ribbon around my neck and, attached to it, the top of the fountain pen. The motion of the horseback ride had caused the pen to become unscrewed and it was out there somewhere on the prairie; my beautiful fountain pen. It is the things we have lost that are sometimes remembered with the greatest poignancy, as I remember my Parker pen.

As for Bessie, when IBM Canada Ltd. placed Joe Fafard's five sculptures of life-sized cows on permanent display on downtown Wellington Street in Toronto, I wrote to the Company to congratulate them and suggested that their cows should be named, as cows always were. I requested that if they were named, would they please call one cow Bessie, and I told them why. I received an appreciative letter, but so far as I know, every cow in that IBM herd remains nameless. A pity.

When a teacher has over thirty students, grades one to ten, he or she cannot give much attention to each grade. In our school there was no after-school activity as farm children had to hurry home to do the interminable chores. But we learned a valuable lesson, how to teach ourselves; one of the main ingredients of education is curiosity and the successful teacher mines that lode, no matter the size or diversity of the class.

There was one other lesson I learned, but it was not part of the curriculum. It was a pleasant spring day and my sisters and I had hitched our horse, Bell, to the buggy for the ride home. As we drove past the entrance to the school, an older student came out onto the front steps. He stood there and smiled at us, well, leered is more like it; a white appendage hung down the front of his dark trousers. We all stared as we drove past but no one said a word. We had just received a graphic lesson on the male anatomy!

Birds – West and East

There were not many wild birds around Saskatchewan farmyards. The large sparrow flocks around the barns would be joined in the winter by snow buntings. On our farm, we had no shelter belt to attract and protect birds.

As a child, I saw a snowy owl once; it sat impassively on the telephone pole near our front door. It was huge, starkly white against the winter sky and certainly the most impressive bird I have seen. It has a 55-inch wingspread. It must have been a particularly cold winter to lure it that far south in search of rodents and rabbits.

In summer, there were crows all over the place. A favourite summer holiday pursuit when we were children was robbing crows' nests in the poplar trees that ringed the sloughs. The nests were built high in the trees and it was a challenge to reach them. Once that was accomplished, the climber would drop the eggs into waiting hands or a can and we would take them home triumphantly to blow. A small hole would be pricked in each end and the trick was to blow out the contents without breaking the shell. Our parents approved of the crows' nest raids, the crows were a nuisance, they ate the young and the eggs of other birds, even tiny chicks were not safe from them. And their raucous calls did nothing to endear them to humans either.

There was a particular slough at the far end of our pasture that attracted many birds in the summer. I wish now that I had had access to a bird book so I could have identified what I was seeing: shore birds, long-legged, short-legged, long-billed, short-billed, they patrolled the edge of the bountiful water for food unmindful of watchers.

Blackbirds sat in the rushes and called to each other: showy male red-winged blackbirds with drab grey mates nearby; tri-coloured blackbirds and the rusty. The blackbird I liked best was the flashy yellow-head. They were not plentiful, somewhat larger (perhaps an optical illusion), but their brilliant yellow heads and necks, in sharp contrast to the black of their bodies, made them exciting to look at.

No doubt about it, the mecca for birds on the prairies was my grandfather's orchard. He had established a shelter belt composed of a variety of trees shortly after taking up his homestead in 1905. I don't know where he obtained the native deciduous trees, but the evergreens had been sent to him from his native Scotland . . . a hundred tiny seedlings. He planted them so they were protected on each side by the hardier Manitoba maples and by poplars. A surprising number survived and to this day, on the deserted farm site, many of the old imported evergreens, with their distinctive yellow bark, are still living. My uncle said he probably destroyed hundreds of small ones over the years, mistaking them for Russian thistle. I salvaged one, taking it home in a jar; it grew to a handsome specimen in the centre of our Saskatoon lawn.

The large shelter belt that my grandparents diligently cared for was an oasis on the barren prairie. No wonder it was a haven for migrating birds; they built their nests, sang their songs, feasted on insects that plagued the fruit trees and berry bushes, and they devoured the fruits and berries nature provided. My Uncle Jim kept a bird book. It had been published in 1923 and Roger Tory Peterson said, when he kindly autographed it for me in 1984 in Toronto, that the same edition had been his first bird book. I sent it to the archives in Regina, Saskatchewan.

There was a path north through the shelter belt to the well that provided water for the house. As children, we would be sent to the well to bring back a pail of water. It was a chore I was reluctant to do; I was terrified of the shrikes that nested nearby. Shrikes shrieked at you, they dove at you menacingly, and what was worse, shrikes caught garter snakes and hung them on the barbs of the wire fence. The combination of shrieking, diving birds and snakes hanging on the barbed wire fence was intimidating in the extreme. No reassurances by my grandparents that the birds wouldn't hurt me and that the snakes were dead, convinced me that the path to the well was a safe place to go. I usually tried to coerce someone, anyone, into accompanying me.

My uncle was especially fond of the colourful orioles and their artfully constructed swinging nests. He would lovingly name the different birds we saw, but, alas, I was too young to appreciate what I was seeing. Two different species, however, were familiar; the lively swallows that built their nest of mud not far from my grandparents house in a shed with an open south side. They were a delight to watch, ever on the move with food for their young. The other birds that were denizens of the barnyard were the pigeons. Obviously my grandparents had obtained a pair years before and in the best tradition of pigeons, they took over. They liked to roost on the barn, dirty and noisy; no-one liked them very much. And how they multiplied! Every now and again my uncle Jim would take his trusty .22 rifle and thin out the flock, an easy target. He would bring several up to my mother and we would 'enjoy' pigeon pie. I didn't like it, but those were the days when food preferences were not encouraged. You ate what was put before you and if you didn't like what was served, you left the table. It was as simple as that.

As children, the most fun of all with the birds was finding their nests in the dense prairie grass. The meadowlarks were a favourite; there were horned larks, too, but not as many. The larks were so clever about hiding their nests it was a triumph to find one.

On our way to school, there was a piece of raw grassland that was a favoured nesting place for the meadowlarks and favourite stopping-off spot for us on the long walk home. After a rain, there would be mushrooms and puffballs everywhere; huge and white they seemed to spring up through the grass over night. We filled our tin lunch pails with mushrooms for our father. My mother would cook them in butter for the evening meal but I had to leave the kitchen as she did; I hated mushrooms, even the smell was intolerable to me. Today I enjoy them but, sadly, the local supermarket does not yield the succulent treasures that grew in abundance on the prairie after a rain.

My husband Henry and I became interested in birding when we bought our first house in Toronto. We had a large window installed in the south entrance overlooking the deep yard. We put glass in the kitchen door and bought swivel chairs so we could bird watch with ease. We had planted many shrubs, bushes and evergreens and like most neophytes from the prairies, we overdid it. Everything seemed to thrive and grow to heights unexpected. It was a natural haven for birds. Two ancient oak trees were at the back of the long lot and they harboured . . . squirrels! These furred black and grey 'friends' became our bird-watching nemesis. They were abetted by a cedar hedge that was there when we bought the house; it extended about twenty feet from the house; a perfect jumping-off place for raiding bird feeders.

We bought a bird book; became knowledgeable about bird seed (and the cost!), and experimented with feeders, particularly feeders that were hostile to squirrels. We soon learned that squirrels chew plastic feeders to pieces and that wood was no deterrent at all. We put the familiar squirrel-barrier metal cones on the posts that held the feeders. Our trouble was basic; squirrels jump . . . and jump . . . and jump. I think we had squirrels that held records for long-distance jumping. They jumped from the cedars, they jumped from the garage roof, they jumped from the back-entrance roof. There seemed nowhere we could put the feeders within our sight-line that was outside the squirrel jumpline. Our lot was narrow, we had too many trees and shrubs. We finally gave up.

In our bird-watching heyday, we carefully recorded the dates of sighting. Our winter of 1980/81 in Toronto lists the following:

> Nuthatches, both red-breasted and white-breasted; evening grosbeaks; juncos; house sparrows and white-throated sparrows; mourning doves; grackles; red-winged blackbirds; blue jays; cardinals; starlings; chickadees; thrushes; downy woodpeckers; robins; cowbirds; crows; pine siskins; goldfinch (banded); flickers; redpolls and a hawk that pounced on the ground-feeding birds and disappeared before it could be identified.

Our most memorable sighting was on January 2, 1979. We had placed the feeder farther back in the yard to try and foil the squirrel invasion. In the early morning I saw a bird on the ground coming toward the house and for a few moments I felt disoriented. I thought "I shouldn't be seeing that bird." My instinct was right; what looked at first glance to be a robin was actually a varied thrush; the black band across its front distinguished it from a robin. I checked our bird book to verify the sighting then phoned Mr. R. Mason who was at the top of the birding pyramid in Toronto. He said he would send someone to investigate. When Mr. Bellerby came the next morning, the thrush was feeding on the ground under the feeder and Mr. Bellerby agreed when he saw it that I was right: it was a varied thrush, the first sighting at a feeder in Toronto. The birding pyramid works as its name indicates, the top man phones two and they in turn phone two others each, thus word spreads. The local *Globe and Mail* daily reported the sighting, giving our address. Even though it was a cold January, birders descended on us from hundreds of miles. We had kept the ground at the base of the feeder free of snow and every morning we replenished the feed. The thrush, a ground feeder, knew a good thing when it saw it so everyone (or almost everyone) could add a varied thrush to their list. Everyone marvelled that such a shy native of forest undergrowth on the west coast had traversed the prairie to arrive safely in Ontario. It stayed until well into April, then we never saw it again. For years we enjoyed making pilgrimages to choice birding sites in Ontario and added to our own list. The only other varied thrush that I saw was in British Columbia when a relative asked me to identify her strange bird!

After the squirrels finally won, we had to content ourselves with binoculars in parks and the back yard. We did, however, put up an attractive little birdhouse, the wood carefully shellacked and a new perch placed under the opening. We hung it on the side of the garage and were gratified when two chickadees decided it was just right. They built their nest inside surprisingly fast and then it seemed no time at all until we heard the plaintive sound of hungry young chickadees. Just when we thought the young would soon appear, we rose one morning to find the birdhouse on the ground, though not broken. All the happy chickadee family, young and old, were gone. The large eyescrew that suspended the birdhouse from the supporting rod had been pulled out, but how? Raccoons . . . a marauding raccoon had lowered itself on to the birdhouse from the garage roof and the weight of the large animal had plunged the chickadee home to the ground. We were in mourning for days. The parent chickadees didn't help; they would flutter through the empty space where their family had been and then huddle disconsolately on the wires nearby, all the while eyeing us with suspicion. We rehung the birdhouse with a stronger hanger but this summer we had no takers. Maybe in the spring.

During our varied thrush period, one of the visitors had said to us, "Now if you can just get us a house finch." House finches are native to California but a small colony had established in New York State. They found Toronto at last. For two summers they nested in a ceiling light fixture on our next door neighbour's front porch. Then a new neighbour took it down. Last summer he hung a large pot of red geraniums from the front of the same porch. The house finches decided they liked the environment so they nested in the geranium. Our neighbour had the tricky problem of keeping the geranium watered without drowning its squatters. All came out well in the end; the wee ones hatched and left the mother geranium in a surprisingly short time; the geranium survived.

House finches are a delight; their lively color and melodious song embellish any place they want to call home, be it a light fixture or red geranium. Perhaps this year, beside the birdhouse, we should hang a bright red geranium on the side of the garage.

Shortly after we moved to Toronto, 'blue jay country', we put up an ornate black plastic bird feeder outside our kitchen window. The usual quota of late-summer avian guests came by for their handouts, among them a blue jay, distinctive because it had a leg that dangled uselessly. It made an attempt to feed from the light-weight feeder that swayed in the wind, but was sadly unsuccessful. The next day the same blue jay appeared again and we noted, without surprise, that the dangling leg was now missing. This time, however, the bird was not alone, it was accompanied by a fellow blue jay. The two settled down together on the feeder perch nearest our window, but only one bird ate: the crippled jay. The other sat quietly beside it, giving the incapacitated bird a prop to lean against so it could feed. The two came to our feeder day after day and repeated the ritual, the crippled one feeding while the other supported it. It was a touching sight, and proof positive that compassion exists in the so-called wild.

Arbor Day

Our one-room school, Ailsa Craig, built 1912, sat on one acre of land beside a main road. The site was not an ideal playground, the north-east corner of it dipped sharply so we never had a level playing field. The schoolyard was fenced, of course, enclosing, as well as the school, a substantial stable and the required outhouses, the boys' south of the stable, the girls' north. A sturdy tall swing near the road and football goal posts, east and west, were the only concession to anything resembling sport.

After a regular school day there was no lingering; horses were quickly hitched and driven straight home, chores waited and they had to be done. But we did have one wild, free day in our schoolyard once a year. It was called Arbor Day, May 23, the day we cleaned up the school yard.

Everybody brought something for the communal lunch, sandwiches, cookies, candy, whatever, and it was stored in one of the cloakrooms until noon. We also came armed with rakes, shovels and any other tool required for the big job.

Everyone, from the grade ones up, was assigned a task and worked hard at it. On Arbor Day a tree should rightly be planted, but planting trees on the prairie was not a casual undertaking. For one thing, saplings have to be kept watered and who would do that in the long, hot holiday summer?

Obtaining a tree to plant was almost an impossibility; the prairie sloughs maintained a fringe of willows and sometimes a grove of poplars, but no one considered a poplar tree one that should or could grace a schoolyard.

So, at least we didn't have to rake leaves on our Arbor Day. But there was plenty of other stuff; dried Russian thistle and tumbling mustard piled up on the fence and in the corners. Dried grasses were raked into piles and, with the thistles and mustard weeds, burned under the careful eye of the teacher. We wore our old clothes and there was much revelry; fun and freedom making light of the work.

On the Arbor Day etched in my memory when I was one of the younger workers, we gathered at noon for lunch. Everything was spread outside on a large makeshift table at one end of which was the big container of water. We needed it, everyone was thirsty. Big plates were piled high with sandwiches, cakes were cut, there were cookies galore, but where was the fudge candy that someone had brought? It was still in the cloakroom. Two girls ran to carry it; it was the size of a cookie sheet. There was a cry of dismay when it was presented, "Where had the candy gone?" or at least a large part of it.

When the teacher demanded to know who had eaten the candy, many small fingers pointed at me and said, "Ina ate it." The teacher had her culprit, so without further ado I was taken into the cloakroom and strapped. It was the only strapping I ever received at school and of course it made a mockery of justice because how could one small girl eat all that candy, but I had to admit that I did eat a bit. So I took the rap. I would like to be able to say that that incident cured me of fudge for life, but I still have a taste for it.

As for the strap, I don't remember if I got one when I got home.

There was a rule in our house: if you got the strap at school, you automatically got one at home...no questions asked. I guess I did.

Two Christmas Trees

The Christmas when I was about eleven, I got the idea that we should have a Christmas tree. It probably had something to do with the Christmas concert at the schoolhouse where the towering Christmas tree was one of the wonders of the evening. I don't know where the tree was obtained but obviously it was brought in from some distance as there certainly were no evergreen trees of that dimension on our part of the prairie where the scraggly poplar tree was king.

The tree at the school had been festooned with tinsel and paper bells and had been lighted with real candles in little metal holders that clipped to the branches. A vigilant attendant with a bucket of water stood inconspicuous guard. But the real eyecatchers were the toys that hung from the branches; these had been provided by proud parents, some of whom were determined not to be outdone. That particular year a gorgeous Eaton Beauty doll was the centrepiece and the focus of all hopeful little-girl eyes. When Santa finally put in his ho-ho appearance and distributed the loot from on and under the tree, the doll was not mine. There were too many girls in our family for one of us to get a doll like that. The gifts we received were invariably sensible: a new game of Snakes and Ladders or a wooden pencil box, perhaps even the three-tiered kind with the sliding lid and sections that swung aside. Anyway it wouldn't be an Eaton Beauty doll, my parents were not given to ostentation.

The imposing tree had given me the idea that I wanted a tree of our own. I announced to my mother one afternoon just before Christmas that I was going out to get one. She indulged me but said to be sure to be home before dark.

The snow was thick like it usually was at that time of year. I dressed warmly and took a sharp knife; I knew just where I was going, to the slough down in the field east of the barn.

It was heavy walking and took longer than I had expected; when

I got there I tramped heavily around the bluff of trees looking for the just right one. The poplar trees were out, too tall, not enough branches. I settled on a piece of a willow tree that looked just about right and tackled it with my knife.

I didn't think it would be that hard to cut. It was awkward trying to cut with my big leather mitts and I was afraid I would drop the knife in the snow and not be able to find it. It was getting late. I finally gave up and looked around in desperation. Then I saw it, a dead willow branch, exactly right. It broke off more easily than I had hoped and I began the long, hard trudge through the deep snow for home. A big white jackrabbit jumped from a hollow by a drift and scared me; I tried to hurry but the heavy willow branch caught in the drifts as I dragged it.

When I finally dragged my snow-covered tree into the kitchen there was a look of dismay and admiration on my mother's face but she entered into the spirit of the thing. After it had dried by the kitchen stove she helped anchor it in the living room by the grama-phone corner on a table; the branches protruded somewhat so we had to break some of them off. Even I had to admit it looked bleak and sparse and not like a real tree at all.

One sister summed it up rather tersely, "A Christmas tree should be green." We asked our mother if she had some green paint but she said she had something even better. I don't know where she found it, but she produced crepe paper, one red, one green and suggested that we wrap the branches with that.

It was fun, one cut the paper in strips, another mixed the flour and water glue to just the right consistency, and then we took turns wrapping every part of it right down to the last twig. There was some controversy about which should be red and which green but when it was finally done, it was the prettiest tree we had ever seen. We had nothing Christmasy to hang on it except three or four tiny red fold-out tissue paper bells. They were just the right touch. We never did get an Eaton Beauty doll. Too bad, today it would be worth close to a thousand dollars.

Our family of six children was not considered large by the stan-dards of the day. Dressing them was something of a challenge, though our mother knitted everything that was knittable, and sewed most of our clothing on her trusty White treadle (until she bought her pride and joy, the more advanced Singer, from a trav-elling salesman). Winter clothing was the big expenditure, as children persisted in growing. My mother devised an ingenious way of coping with 'good winter coats' for both our sister, Lois, and her brother, John, five years younger. She ordered a double-breasted, navy blue wool coat, then sewed large black hooks on the inside hem, and the hook eyes higher up on the lining. Lois wore the coat as is, but John could also wear it, with the hem hooked up shorter and the buttoning reversed.

It annoyed our mother that her mother (our grandmother), did not rejoice when another little Gifford was on the way. Her mother would say, "Not again, Isabel," when the fact was that they had identical families: four girls and two boys; at least that is how it was until Iris came, but our grandmother was deceased by then and could not tut-tut over the seventh Gifford.

Getting us all ready for the big Christmas school concert was no picnic. One year I was to be centre stage because I had a recitation to do. I was rehearsed well at home and was all set to go when my mother saw, to her dismay, that my Buster Brown bangs were badly in need of cutting. My father was pressed into hurried action and the sharp shears were soon shearing. My mother came into the kitchen to check the progress and was horrified to find that my bangs now extended from ear to ear. A new style in Buster Brown haircuts was initiated that night!

(I do not recall who had the honour of wearing the navy blue coat to the concert, Lois or John.) And neither do they.

Wells

My father was one of those rare people who could successfully witch for water; this talent was well utilized by friends and neighbours. It was summer, usually a nice Sunday morning, when he got the urge to witch, or perhaps a neighbour had phoned to say he needed another well.

I went with him to a nearby slough as he carefully selected just the right willow branch. It had to be a live branch (no dead wood), forked (absolutely essential), large enough for a good grip and just the right length. All cuts would be made at an angle.

After he had carefully prepared his Y-shaped instrument, the positioning of the hands was important: he grasped each forked branch with his fingers facing outward and the prong of the branch pointing upwards. He would then walk with the witch held straight out in front, slowly, slowly, giving it time to locate its mark. The pull of the underground water was irresistible, the upright prong of the Y would be drawn down with such compelling force that I have seen the green bark of the forked branches forced loose even in his tight grasp.

We had three wells on our farm: one near the old barn, another at the top of the hill near the big barn, and another in the pasture, all with differing qualities of water.

My mother used the old well to keep food cool in the summer. A container would be lowered to just above the water. While it was not a refrigerator, or even an ice box, it sufficed. Refrigerators were luxuries in the far future and we had no ice house as some farmers had. Thick ice for the ice house had to be harvested from a slough in the winter and then stored in the ice house between protective layers of straw. The ice sometimes lasted into July until the intense prairie heat took its toll.

The old well at the back of the house had no cover and every summer it would be the target for suicide-prone young turkeys. Turkeys, as almost everyone knows, are prone to suicide; they seriously lack a will to live. When the young ones tried to fly up to roost on the side of the well, they ineptly misgauged the distance and down they went into the twenty-foot-deep well. When retrieved, my mother would wrap a towel around the dazed bird, place it on the open door of the kitchen stove oven but usually to no avail: exit turkey. The good well at the top of the hill, not far from the barn, provided the water for humans and animals. My father had tapped into a strong underground spring and the quality of that clear, ice-cold water makes me thirsty to remember. The well was about thirty-six feet deep, an open well with no pump nor cover, the top of the cribbing about level with the top of the horse trough.

My father had constructed a windlass that we turned by hand to raise the big bucket of water. He had devised the pail, a straight sided metal container with a content about two and a half times that of an ordinary pail. On the bottom of the bucket there was a hinged trap that opened when it hit the water and closed when the bucket was lifted. It was very efficient, but very heavy, especially for the child-strength that was expected to operate it. One of the most difficult parts of the operation was maneuvering the big bucket over the side of the well to fill the kitchen pails or the horse trough.

In the summer, it was the children's duty to fill the big galvanized iron trough before the horses came in from work in the field; my father did not want the heated horses drinking ice-cold water from the well. It took a lot of buckets to fill the trough; our hands would blister from turning the heavy winch handle.

Summer at the well was one thing, winter quite an other. We did not have to keep the trough full in winter, but on occasion when we were sent to the well for drinking water, it was a hazardous adventure indeed. Ice, formed from spilled and dripping water, built up and around the well casing until it was level with the top. We had to stand on the slippery slope of it to operate the windlass. One small misstep and we would have slid into the well. It did not seem to occur to any adult to chop away the ice to provide less precarious footing. But then, child safety was rarely a factor on a working farm.

The well in the pasture was not deep; I recall one occasion when I was tempted to jump into it to escape an enraged cow, but that's another story. There was a surprising variance in the quality of the waters my father witched. I know of one well for my aunt, his sister, who was our neighbour, in which the water was an opaque reddish color with a peculiar odour. Upon being submitted for analysis, it was determined to be 'Five hundred times removed beyond human consumption.' The analysis did not reveal what elements it contained, perhaps a fortune lurked under the prairie soil! Of course my father did not apologize, he witched for water quantity, quality was not guaranteed.

Brandon Marquis 7th

The animal, wild or domesticated, that is responsible for more deaths in the world to humans is the farm bull. After living with Brandon Marquis 7th, I believe that.

Brandon Marquis 7th was the community bull and we kept him.

He was introduced by the Department of Agriculture to improve the cattle quality in our district. The Government supplied the bull; in this instance they made bad mistakes, as governments are prone to do. Mark, as we called him, was a Shorthorn through and through. He was a magificent animal, true to his breeding. He weighed about a ton, was an attractive roan color and had one significant feature that contributed a great deal to his threatening demeanour: he had thick, sharply pointed horns. My father had been assured before he went to pick him up at the CNR station in Harris, that he had been dehorned. Indeed, he had not. Rumour had it that he had once killed a keeper and, looking at him, it was not hard to believe that it was true. The government had made another mistake, the mistake of sending a superb beef animal into a district whose prime need was milk. For years after, Mark made his mark on the cattle herds in our district, we had high quality beef but a definite reduction of cream to churn into butter.

My father made arrangements for Mark's arrival by building a corral the length of the eastern side of the barn. It was a generous size and was constructed of wood telephone poles, shortened, but tall enough to accommodate many strands of closely spaced heavy barbed wire. The gate, which swung inward past the side of the barn, was built from criss-crossed planks and was secured by a heavy chain that fastened with a massive buckle on the outside of the post next to the barn wall. It was a formidable enclosure for a formidable animal.

Farmers from a wide area brought their cows to Mark for servicing; the charge was 50 cents per cow, my father's pay. He kept a careful record of all Mark's services, a government requirement.

In the winter, Mark was kept in a box stall in the barn. He was fastened by a heavy halter; there was a ring through his nose. My father would lead him outside to the water trough on occasion, using a wood staff with a device on the end that could be opened by a rope to lock or unlock the staff into the nose ring.

When Mark's hooves needed cutting, my father would enlist the help of a brave neighbour. He would place a big washtub of oats in front of the animal and together he and the neighbour would saw the hooves, working against time while the hungry animal was preoccupied with eating. It was a risky business.

In the summer, when Mark became bored in his pen, my father would assuage the boredom by throwing an old garment over the fence into the corral. Then it was a sight (and sound) to behold. Mark would roar in rage as he pawed and scraped and used his great horns to shred the garment that carried the hated human smell. It was reciprocated, all of us feared and hated Mark.

One nice summer day I had been sent up to the well for water for the kitchen. The well was deep and the pail was heavy. As I struggled with the windlass to bring the pail to the surface, I heard a strange sound. I knew right away it was Mark. The well and the trough were enclosed by a northern and eastern solid wood windbreak. It was about eight feet high and obstructed my view of Mark's pen. I knew right away that something was wrong; Mark was making a sound I had never heard from him before. I tried to hurry with the water pail but my 12-year-old strength was inadequate for hurrying. Finally, when the pail was safely on the ground, I ran around the corner of the shelter to see what was happening. With horror I saw immediately that Mark was opening his gate. The sound he was making was an eerie combination of excitement and triumph. The fact that the gate swung inward toward him was my salvation. The big lock that secured the chain on the outside had broken and he was using his horns to try to pull the gate inward far enough to let him go free. No wonder he was so excited.

I did the only thing I could do, I dashed over to the gate, grabbed it and pulled it back shut against the pole. He tried to stop me. He pushed a horn through next to my hand, but I was able to get the end of the chain around the pole and I hung on to it for dear life. He tried hooking his horn around a gate plank to get a hold so he could drag the gate in. The thing that prevented him from doing so was that his horns were smooth and straight so they slid off the plank; had they been bent he might have succeeded. All the while he was making the deep, menacing sound that had alerted me in the first place. I had never been so close to the huge animal before and I was almost paralyzed by fear. The hatred in his eyes was palpable as we stood face to face and wrestled for control of the gate.

I thought of my brothers and sisters playing innocently in the yard at the foot of the hill and knew the awful fate that awaited them if Mark got free. My father was plowing a long furrow, east to west, that I could not see; it was down the steep hill out of range of my sight. I knew that sooner or later the plow would reach the top of the hill; I had to hold on to the chain. It was no use to call for help, the house was too far away for anyone to hear and I had not been gone long enough for my mother to worry.

I will never forget the sight of the horses' ears bobbing up over the hill. I did not scream or call out as I did not want to do anything to further rouse the ire of the enraged bull.

My father came running as soon as he saw me; I suppose the absolute terror on my face made him realize something dreadful was wrong. It was his turn to hold the chain while I ran to get a piece of wire so he could safely secure it.

At last some other district needed Mark; it was such a relief to see him go and we never again had a bull at our farm.

My father took Mark to town one Fall day after loading him into a wagon and securing him by the nose ring to a fastener on the floor. He went alone, which was rather foolish. He underestimated the weight of the huge animal, the steepness of the Eagle Creek hill, and he overestimated the strength of the team of horses. Apparently, on the way up the long hill the horses, who had travelled many miles by then, almost gave up. The tired team strained to keep the wagon on course. There was real danger; the weight of the bull if he swayed would throw the wagon off balance and possibly tip it, with disastrous results. My father stopped the horses part way up out of the creek bed, got out and placed large rocks from the side of the road behind the wheels. The rocks held.

When he finally pulled in to the railroad station, the men there could hardly believe that he had transported the massive animal all by himself. I wonder if he told them how close it had been to becoming a disaster.

Aftermath: For years I have had night terrors of being chased by a bull but the bull in my dream is not Mark, it is always a white-headed Hereford stranger, but equally vengeful.

My Father

What should I write about my father? I don't know. He was handsome, and, like most sons who are handsome, he was doted on by his mother. When you knew the family structure, you could understand why. She had had too many girls and a handsome son, at last, was to be cherished. Handsome men, who have been spoiled by their mothers, expect their wives and daughters, to do the same. So it was with my father. Knowing this, did not make living with him any easier; a child does not have the perspective to understand the idiosyncracies of its parents. Even at this remove, I still find it difficult to find my perspective. It is said that a man is either a good father or a good husband, but rarely both.

My father was not a good and kind father to me, and I am not sure he was a good husband, either. He was born in 1885, into a family that stemmed from United Empire Loyalists. He was clever, but once again, like clever spoiled sons, his mother had been lenient when it came to teaching him self-discipline. My father's parents came west to live with him on his homestead in Saskatchewan which he claimed in 1909. His father, who had been born in 1828, died in 1910; his mother, born in 1845, died in 1938.

My father had not intended to stay on the prairie farm any longer than was required to prove up his homestead. He would then sell it, he thought, and get out with a nice pile of money. He was not the only young man who took out a homestead with that idea in mind. But it did not work out that way, at least for my father. He married, had children, and settled down to the life that such responsibilities dictate. His nature was not that of a farmer. He was a young man who had enjoyed a carefree life, free to roam, take employment to sustain him for the moment, and then move on. He was twenty-three when he decided to take advantage of the opportunities that Western Canada afforded. The die for him, with that decision, had been cast.

My father had a sister, Henrietta, whom we called Aunt Hat, who had taken out a homestead adjoining her brother's. She was fifteen years older than he and I think their incompatability stemmed from that difference in age; she had an older sister bossiness that he found aggravating, understandably. My reason for mentioning this is that I physically resembled my Aunt Hat and I feel that fact had a large bearing on my parents' attitude toward me. I was the second girl, a year and a half younger than Jean, the first born. Jean was the apple of their eyes. My sister, Lois, remarked not long ago that our father only had two children: the oldest, Jean, and the youngest, Iris. I think there was an element of truth in that. The five in between were tolerated, barely.

Jean and I were two different people: she was Miss Goody Two-Shoes, and I was not. Jean had blonde, curly hair, mine was straight and dark. In the snapshots my mother took of us both, Jean is always front and centre, with her lovely blonde hair tied with a beautiful big bow. If I am in the picture, time and again I am cut off, half there, an appendage; in one picture the dog, Carlo, is trying to lick my sticky face, while Jean sits primly nearby, disdaining to recognize us.

Our Aunt Hat took exception to the disparity of treatment shown to the two of us by our parents. She spoke once of an incident she had witnessed that illustrated her point. A neighbour had come for his mail just after we had come home from school; Jean was in grade three and I in grade two. My father, to show how well Jean was doing in school, asked her an oral arithmetic question. Before she answered, I did, correctly. My father was annoyed my aunt recalled, he slapped me across the face and said, "Nobody asked you." In a typical scenario, Jean practised the violin while I was sent to feed the pigs. If I resented it at the time, it was only mildly, but of course the discrepancy in treatment showed up as we got older.

When my father came in from the field, he was no sooner in the yard with the horses than he was shouting, "Ina." He did not seem to want to do much without me standing by helping. He was a fine carpenter, who had built or helped build most of the buildings in our district. He had an impressive array of tools; I had to know the names and uses of every one so I could hand him the correct tool. I recall on one occasion I was helping him put up a partition in a granary. We were handling a long plank. He told me to turn it end for end. I did not know what he meant and that brought a torrent of abuse down on my head, so severe I remember the humiliation to this day. Instead of explaining to me what he meant, he treated me as if I were a moron. He was intolerant and impatient, especially where I was concerned.

We were all afraid of my father. I do not know what kind of relationship my parents established in the early years of their married life, but I do know that my mother was not the kind to back down to anyone. She indulged my father, as his mother had done, up to a point. He was not good at managing money, but she, a Scot, was, so the burden of handling the family finances fell to her. The money that she earned for boarding the teacher and for running

Above: John Elder sod house built 1905. Note the two essentials: water barrel on left, poplar wood drying on the right.

Right: Mother, Isabel Hamilton Elder, age 21.

Below: Mr. and Mrs. John Elder with (from left) Janet (Ettie), James (Jim), John Jr., and Bessie, 1922.

Left: John Elder, Sr. and Mrs. Ed. Jones, Bents railway station.
Above: Jim Elder at home.

Middle: Ed Gifford's parents: Henry Gifford, 1828-1910; Kezia Anne Gifford, 1845-1938.
Left: Ed Gifford's sister, Harriet Ashton, 1870-1958.
Right: Teacher George Lyon and Ed Gifford, right.

Above: Jim Elder and sisters harvesting with oxen.

Left: Elders' tractor-drawn combine.

Below: Enclosed sleigh heated by coal burning stove. Neighbour coming to Gifford home for mail.

The Elders' oxen pulling a wagon.

AUCTION SALE

Car

Separator

Engine

Horses

Implements

Etc.

PROPERTY OF THE ESTATE OF THE LATE

John Elder Sr.

Will be held on the North West of 12-33-13, One mile South of Bents

ON

THUR. APRIL 6

Commencing at 1 o'clock sharp

STOCK

One Horse 7 yrs. old.   Horse 16 ys old.   Mare 9 yrs. old.   Mare 17 yrs. old.   Horse 3 yrs. old, unbroken

FARM IMPLEMENTS

One Seeder, 20 run	One Binder, 8 foot cut	One Cultivator	One Mower and Hay Rake
One 14 in. Gang Plow,	One 16 in, Sulky Plow	Two Grain Wagons	One Set of Drag Harrows
Two Sleighs	Two Trucks and Racks	One 10 foot Packer	One 8 foot Tandem Disc
One Pump Engine	One Buggy	One Cutter	One 4 Bottom Engine Plow
SOME HARNESS	ONE OLD McLAUGHLIN CAR	1-4 SHARE IN GEORGE WHITE SEPARATOR	

TERMS CASH

Auctioneer, T. L. MAJOR, Tessier

Auction Sale poster, April 6, 1931.

	Wood Harrow	W Ridgewell	6 . 00
	Harrow Cart	"	4 . 00
Tandem	Dix Harrow	J Liska	22 . 00
	Seeder	John Elder	35 . 00
	Mower	W. H. Bottomly	14 . 00
	Rake	James Elder	13 . 00
	Binder	Guy Rossworm	45 . 00
	Wagon	R. D. Clayton	45 . 00
	Wagon	W. H. Bottomly	20 . 00
	Wagon & Rack	Paul Steves	22 . 00
	Wagon & Rack	R D. Clayton	20 . 00
	Sleigh (steel)	W Laing	9 . 00
	Sleigh (cast)	James Elder	13 . 00
	Engine Plow	John Elder	10 . 00
½ share	Separator	John Elder	50 . 00
	Car	R. D. Clayton	28 . 00
	Cutter	James Elder	20 . 00
	Buggy	J. A. Adams	25 . 00
	Pump Engine	James Elder	9 . 00
½ set	Harness	W. Wardrope	4 . 00
Full set	Harness	James Elder	15 . 00
	Breeching	W Hiscock	5 . 00
	Set Harness	Paul Steve	10 . 00
½ set	Harness	W Bottomley	3 . 00
Full set	Harness	W Bottomley	12 . 00
3	Bridles	John Mair	3 . 00
light driving	Harness	Frank Clayton	8 . 00

Horses

Mare	Biddy (17) –	John Elder	45 . 00
"	Legs (10) –	R. D. Clayton	65 . 00
Horse	Charlie (6)	John Elder	30 . 00
"	Sandy (9)	James Elder	72 . 00
Colt .	Colt (3)	" "	65 . 00

Sale of effects at John Elder Sr. auction.

THE
SASKATCHEWAN GRAIN GROWERS'
ASSOCIATION
INCORPORATED

AILSA CRAIG G. G. ASSN.
E. B. GIFFORD, Sec. Treas.

ORGANIZATION EDUCATION
AND CO-OPERATION WILL BRING THE
FARMER INTO HIS OWN

PICHE, Sask.,

Mch 2 7th 1922

Dear mama I am aut of bed I am very happy.
I am nat gaing to schoal. Ill soon be gaing to
schoal. I want to go to schoal me and jan
bring up the patatase for grama.
One day we peeled the patatase for grama.
gradma took spats sheep skin away. bekus
spat wet it. Eva and jais are very happy.
I wer my red dress at ham. it is very
warm. I sleep with dady I like to slup
with dady. I read my primer lats.
I wasnt aut sid far a long time.
it has been very cold I like to be up.
I write on the beack bord lats.
haw is the laty. be shoor you get a
dalls haid. haw are you fuling.
cecl brings in the eggs. thank you
From Ina

Letter written by Ina, age 6, to her mother, who was in Saskatoon awaiting the birth of Ted. He was born April 3, 1922. See picture of Ina and 2-month old Ted on opposite page.
Elaborate letterheads such as the one shown here are now sought by collectors.

Above left: May 23, 1922. Ina holding brother Ted.
Above right: Father and Iris, age 7, shortly before she left for Scotland in Spring 1939.
Below: Summer slough fun. Lois, left, Ina and Jean, right.

Above: Mother, Isabel Gifford, with Jean, age 2, and Ina age 8 months.

Right: Father, Ed Gifford with Jean, age 6, Ina, age 4, Lois, age 2 and Carlo the dog, 1920.

Above: Jean, Ina, Lois, Eva, Edward, John – The Gifford family, 1928.

the post office, was hers and she used it to good purpose. We were lucky children to have her at the helm. There was one occasion, though, when she let me down. It was a mid-summer day and I have no recollection of what might have sent my volatile father into one of his furies. All I recall is being knocked down on the sere, yellow grass near the house while my father beat me with a whip. The whip he used had been cut from the rim of a Model T tire. It was flexible, sharply triangular, with three cutting edges. It lashed my slight body without mercy until I finally fell into unconsciousness.

When I came to, I was in our mother's bed and she was rubbing vaseline into the welts on my back. I was surprised, she was crying. Crying over me! Today I am not sure if she was crying because I had been hurt, or if she cried because she feared her husband could be charged with murder, which was punishable by hanging then. I prefer to think she was crying over me. My sisters had witnessed the attack and I had never considered the effect on them until a few years ago when Lois raised the subject. Something had been said about our mother and Lois said, "I hate her." I was shocked and remonstrated with her, "Why would you ever say that?" Her reply surprised me, "Because she never defended you."

My father's fits of fury were unpredictable. One nice summer morning my sister, Jean, and I watched in transfixed horror as our father beat a poor cow almost to death with an iron bar. She had moved a leg as he was milking her. We were standing in the barn door waiting to take the cow to the pasture after he was done and we did not notice her transgression. It was an appalling sight which no child should have had to witness; I have tried to push it to the back of my consciousness but, at the most unexpected moments, it returns to haunt me.

Why did we not run and get our mother to try to stop him, I will never know. Perhaps we were afraid that if we tried to intervene, he would wreak his wrath on us too. So we huddled and watched, and I never forgave him. The cow survived, but he soon parted with her. He told the buyer that another animal had attacked her. He was right! I am grateful that the bad habit our father had of hitting us on the side of the head did not damage our brain.

My sister Jean, recalling our father's vicious and unpredictable temper, said about his mental and physical abuse of me, "He needed that outlet." Fine for her to say! I think it was because I resembled his sister, Harriet; I was the surrogate for his dislike. As for my mother, sometime in the early years of parenthood, they had determined that if one was imposing discipline, the other would not interfere. It was probably sensible, but in my case it was carried to extremes.

That my father was a dictator is undisputed, but that was the role of the head of the household when he was young. After all, in Canada, women were not legally persons until 1929. It is easy to exercise control over someone who does not even have the legal status of being considered a person. No wonder women have had to work hard to extract any concessions, legally, from males.

I had a small taste, in the early 1960's of what some women had been up against. I had written productions for the CBC when I lived in Saskatchewan. When I came to Toronto, I naturally assumed that my talents would be recognized. I applied for a position with the CBC as a writer. After all, my work needed no introduction.

When I kept my appointment with the head of the creative department, he sat across from me, his big shiny desk between us, and said to me, quite frankly, "We could not possibly hire you, all of our writers are young men." He would not dare say that so bluntly today, but I have a feeling that the end result could be the same, but couched in more 'sensitive' language.

When my granddaughter, Lindsay, said to me that she was not a feminist, I did not let her remark pass. I explained to her that the freedoms she took for granted had been hard won by women who had preceded her. In the case of my father, the construct of the family worked in his favour. To have a wife and four dutiful daughters, made him king and he took full advantage of his position. One time he surprised us, though. He had just come home after a stint of work in the city. It was Sunday, we were enjoying a lunch around the dining room table together. Ordinarily, my father would just indicate by a gesture that his teacup was empty. That day he got up from the table, went to the kitchen, and filled his teacup by himself. We all looked at him in amazement, nothing like that had ever happened before. Why should he do anything for himself when he had so many females at his command? It didn't last, of course, he soon reverted to the old, dictatorial ways.

I think having so many daughters before he had two sons contributed to my father's attitude toward women. When, after our mother died at age 41, the boys Ted and John, became youths, then young men, his control over them was modified. He did not expect as much from his sons as he did from his daughters. But then, his dependence on his beloved "Tot" had never been so evident until after she was gone. First, he was his mother's son, then Tot was there to continue to spoil him. No daughter took over their role.

Life is full of ironies, one of the ones in my life was the fact that my father seemed to feel, when I was an adult with children of my own, that I owed him more than the others. I was the one he tried to lean on, the one he turned to for help and support. After the farm was sold, he went to the city, Saskatoon, where I was working and immediately looked to me for help, just as he had always called my name when he drove the horses into the farmyard, "Ina." I resisted. My sister, Jean, was married and living in Regina. She would write and tell me how I should care for our father. Lois was in far off Vancouver, her husband's mother lived with them. The boys were involved in lives of their own. Traditionally, it has been the females in the family who have provided the comfort and succour. In a letter my father had written to his sister in California, he mentioned my name, "I don't know what Ina thinks of me." To tell the truth, I don't know what I thought of him, either. Filial love runs deep, but it is tempered by the sad memories of injustice. That is what made me ambivalent about my father. I was with him when he died in 1959 at the age of 74. He had developed prostate cancer, but would not agree to an operation. "Going under the knife," is what he called it, and he was adamant about not doing that. As I was the only one of his children in the city, I went to the hospital daily, baked the chocolate cake he liked, and tried to do the things for him that my sister, Jean, thought I should! He did not last long. At one point he asked me "What is my position?" I lied and said, "You're doing fine, Dad."

In his final hours, I was alone with him; I read passages from the Bible that I knew he favoured, crying as I read. Finally, as I held his hand, he expired, and as he did so, I felt his soul caress mine as it left his body. So maybe I found favour in his sight in the end, just maybe.

Everything I have said has involved my personal relationship with my father. So far as the rest of the world is concerned, he was a clever man, interested in the governance of the country and of the world. He was active in politics, and received the Federal nomination for our rural riding, under the banner of the Liberal Progressive party. He did not win, we did not go to Ottawa; I suspect my mother was secretly relieved. At one time, the Imperial Oil Company had asked him to come on board, but my mother vetoed it. She probably did not want to submit him to the lures of city life. After all, he was handsome, gregarious and well spoken. I think she thought it better to keep him to herself in the country. She may have been right. My father was offended by any abuse of the Western farmer. One year, when the Massey-Harris binder broke down, once too often, and threatened the success of the harvest, my father wrote to the president of the company and told him it was a sin to produce machinery of such shoddy construction. The president replied, with some asperity, and told my father in no uncertain terms, that his company was in business for the benefit of their shareholders, and not for the glory of God.

My father wrote articles that were published in the dailies, suggesting changes in legislation that would benefit the farmers. He was one of a group responsible for bringing Mr. Aaron Shapiro to the province to help form the Saskatchewan Wheat Pool, a marketing organization badly needed at the time. He was also, at one time, the secretary of the United Grain Growers' Association. I have a letter on their elaborate letterhead that I wrote to my mother when she was in the hospital in Saskatoon in 1922. I was six years old. She had gone to the hospital to give birth to my brother Edward (Ted). After four girls, success at last! When strangers enquired about the size of his family, my father would proudly reply, "I have four daughters and every one of them has a brother." Ted was the one they had aspired to have from the beginning, but once again, as happens so often in life, the timing was off.

When Ted and his younger brother, John, who was born in 1923, grew old enough to work on the land, my father had no land of his own left to till; the mortgage company took it over. Neither son stayed on the land. The pioneer days were over.

 The Land

What a difference four years made to a man looking for a homestead on the prairies. When my grandfather Elder located his in 1905, he found land that was flat and fertile . . . no sandy soil, no stones, no alkali, even a couple of fair-sized sloughs. When my father came after, just four years later, he had to settle for land that was not so desirable. From the flat, easily tilled land that was my grandfather's (and his two sons' who took out adjoining homesteads) the prairie terrain rose gradually to the north. A mile north of the Elders' it started to become contoured, rolling land which gradually became knolls, then hills that were more sharply vertical, more pronounced, until they finally ended in an extended, high formation called the Bear Hills. My father's homestead was about three miles south of the Bear Hills. His land was hilly, so hilly in fact that when he tried to cultivate it later with a huge steam engine, the behemoth could not navigate many of the steep hills. But it was good land, no sandy soil, no stones; but we did have alkali sloughs.

I often wonder what possessed my father to erect his homestead buildings where he did. A section of land (640 acres) was a mile square and he had the two eastern quarters of the section. Three-hundred-and-twenty acres was about the maximum that could be tilled by one man using horses. Road allowances were along the perimeters of the section but instead of sensibly locating by the road, he built a half mile in. As a result, our house sat almost on the dividing line between my father's quarter sections and his sister's. Aunt Hat (Harriet) had taken the west half of the section and had built her house on the road allowance to the west. The awkward positioning of our homestead meant that we had to take a meandering trail across our fields to reach the buildings. The big barn was built on the top of a very steep hill and was visible for miles. The house was built further down the west slope. But there was another disadvantage to the siting of the buildings; they were directly between two large alkali sloughs, one to the north and the other to the south. They were the only alkali sloughs on our land and he built directly between them! On certain summer days the stench from them was almost intolerable, depending from which direction the wind blew. Once smelled, never forgotten!

My dictionary definition of alkali soil: "Soil that has either a high degree of alkalinity or a high percentage of sodium, or both, so that most common crops cannot be grown on it profitably." What an innocuous description of alkali. The dictionary did not mention alkali sloughs, on which *nothing* will grow! On the margins a short red succulent turned brown and prickly as it matured and had no food value.

Alkali sloughs on the prairies were dangerous. The dark grey sticky mass with a slick of water on top was sometimes attractive to cattle, I don't know why, possibly for the sodium. Cattle, or other large animals, did not need to get far into it before they became completely bogged down and unable to move. I remember one spring when a lovely young heifer ventured into the treacherous morass with fatal results. She frantically tried to extricate herself, but even when my father and her owner tried to pull her out using a team of horses stationed on dry land, it was no use.

In the summer heat, the alkali water would dry up and a hard, cracked crust would form on top, but there was still the sludge underneath; if we got it on our feet it was very difficult to wash off.

Alkali soil soon destroyed all vestiges of any prey, thus it was the burial site for our old work-worn horses. My father would lead them down to the edge of the north slough and shoot them. I am sure it must have been a traumatic experience for him but was part of the downside of being a horse farmer.

It was a paradox that the sourer the alkali slough, the sweeter the soil seemed to be that surrounded it. One slough I recall (where the heifer died), was a big one, south of my aunt's; the north-south road past her house could not possibly have been built through it so the road skirted the slough completely except at the very western end. There, in bypassing the alkali slough, it isolated a small normal slough. That little slough was a source of fascination for me in the summertime on my way to and from school – we went to school in August. It would be alive with water birds, long legs, long bills, strange calls. Of course I had no idea what I was seeing, but I would lie on my stomach in the tall grasses and reeds by the edge of the slough and bird watch. No bird was ever seen in or on an alkali slough, but on this sweet little slough they revelled in the feed and the water.

I am not sure exactly when the surveying of the prairies was done, but I do know that it was the largest area in the world ever surveyed as a unit; a gigantic operation.

Survey markers were placed at the corners of every square-mile section. The markers consisted of four two-foot squares dug in a pattern to form a larger square, the sides indicating precise east, west, north and south directions. At the very centre of the square pattern, a numbered marker, a sturdy metal stake, was driven into the soil. Being mischievous children, we tried to pull out the marker stakes; a serious infraction of the law had we been able to do so.

The rich, loam soil worked by the prairie pioneers required two elements: heat and moisture, but those two elements were at the mercy of capricious Nature. The first prairie farmers, without benefit of technology or chemicals, lived on hope and their faith that the right moisture and the right heat would be provided. Sometimes they were, but more often they were not. The prairie farmer knew the meaning of the warning "Beware of the furrow that shines." The furrow that shone could dry solid and hard and require much work before it was broken into tillable soil. I remember vividly the sound of the furrow being turned as I walked behind the breaking plow on a virgin quarter my father had rented. It was the sound of resistant roots being torn asunder, particularly the roots of the wild rose. Rose roots were heavy and white and they seemed to fight hard against the sharp blade that was inflicted upon them. No one knows how long they had endured; Canadian prairie soil is older then the soil of the Nile in geological reckoning. The intrusion of the breaking plow was a breakthrough of no mean dimension.

The Bear Hills that filled our northern horizon and extended somewhat to the east and the west were a big influence on our lives. They not only limited our horizons but also our areas of social intercourse which, of necessity, were directed toward the southerly town of Harris.

Actually, a hardy soul or two did try to make a home in the forbidding hills. A distant cousin of the Elder family, Willie James Wilson, took out a homestead and tried to eke out a living from the poor soil; it took a character such as Willie Wilson to undertake to subdue The Bear Hills. He was a remittance man, of whose ilk there were quite a few on the prairies. Willie had emigrated from Scotland where his father was rumoured to be a doctor. I only visited his shack once when I was a child and my Uncle Jim drove up by horse and buggy to take Willie reading material. I don't remember much about his wooden shack but I do remember his barn and his obvious love of his horses which he treated like pets. Why he had been packed off to the ends of the earth, Canada, I do not know, nor even that he was a true remittance man. As the term indicates, remittance men received remittances on the condition that they stay far away and not embarrass their family at home.

Willie Wilson must have ventured from his home in The Hills because I have postcards that he mailed from a CNR train as it journeyed in 1911 through the Rockies to the west coast. He sent each of the three Elder girls a postcard; he did not play favourites. The interesting thing about the postcards so far as collectors are concerned is that they were bought on the train from the 'newsie' and had been produced for that purpose. Newsie postcards were all in a numbered series and serious collectors try to complete the series. Willie's had been mailed from the train mail car en route as the cancellations show an RPO (railway post office) that vouches to their authenticity. About Willie, I don't know when, or under what circumstance, he left his farm in The Hills. Archeologists who have made a study of The Hills and mentioned his sojourn there may know. My father had seen stones there in formations that indicated places of gathering and worship. Apparently, from the artifacts discovered, researchers have determined the number of tribes that lived there (six) and their probable sequence.

Sometimes in the summer, when rain was sparse, my father would drive up into The Hills with a team and wagon loaded with empty barrels to fill with soft water from a large slough that was not on the fenced community range where the cattle ranged for the summer. Water for the animals was supplied by windmills or from sloughs. Cowboys on horseback were cautioned not to dismount as the animals could become feral.

The spring water from our deep well by the barn was what was known as hard; that meant that soap curdled in it so it was almost impossible to get a clean wash. My mother would dump a can of lye into a barrel of well water, but there was nothing like genuine soft water for a good wash, both for humans and for their clothes.

The Hills were scary when I was young because that's where the coyotes lived. We knew coyote packs lived there because their prolonged eerie howls reverberated from hill to hill on summer evenings, striking fear in the hearts of children miles away. Reassurances that they would not hurt us fell on deaf ears.

The Hills, after a dry summer, could be very dramatic. A prairie fire would start and, depending on the thickness and dryness and the wind direction, it would sweep through The Hills sending acrid smoke toward us; it provided quite a scene, especially after dark, that was like a giant stage setting of destruction. The contours of the hills would be outlined in flames and we would watch in awe as they transformed our horizon; a sight never to be forgotten.

As with most things in life, you have to personally experience things to really appreciate them. Strangers driving through the flat lands of south Saskatchewan refer to it as boring. As a child, I found our land enchanting, from the deep footpaths in the pasture that had been made by buffalo as they made their thirsty way to what was now our south pasture slough, to their skulls that littered the pasture knolls. It was fun to try to find one that still had the horns in it so we could pull them out and show our mother our trophies. I loved the little yellow violets that grew in just one place, on the side of a pasture hill. Years later I went to that hill to try to salvage some of the rare violets for propagation, but, alas, the pasture was now a cultivated field. The violets were gone forever, just like the buffalo, from that favoured land.

But one thing is still there: the big barn high on it's hill. Long may it reign!

Aunt Hat

Harriet Llewellyn Gifford, 1870-1958, my father's sister, fifteen years older than he, farmed the half-section adjacent to ours. She was a woman born out of her time; a woman who not only took out a homestead, but worked her own land.

Aunt Hat, as we called her, was a tall, handsome woman, lovely figure, beautiful hair. She had always been at odds with convention.

As a young woman, she travelled extensively in her home provinces, the Maritimes, earning her living as a photographer, a vocation unusual for women at that time. But that was Aunt Hat. She liked quality, favoured well-bred horses and dogs. This was evident as she travelled in her fine rig, accompanied by a striking pair of dalmatians. Naturally, she was an excellent photographer, and a good business woman. So what was someone of her character doing working a homestead in Saskatchewan? It was the old familiar story: money; she saw an opportunity to make it. At that time in Canada's history (World War I) there was a campaign to encourage farmers, western farmers in particular, to grow wheat for the allies, so she considered it a patriotic gesture. Aunt Hat had been married when she was young to a 'Mr. Black.' But the union had dissolved by the time her gesture of patriotism took her to the prairies.

My father and Aunt Hat had many siblings, including the 'half' variety. Their father, Henry Gifford, had been born in 1828. He married in the Maritimes, had a family of four and after his wife died, married again. The second wife, Kezia Ann Colpitt of New Brunswick, was much younger than her husband, seventeen years younger to be exact; not much older than her step-children. Kezia Ann was a treasure: she not only sewed her husband's suits, she sheared the sheep, spun the wool, dyed it, wove it, cut the garment (without a pattern) and tailored it. Her family (from United Empire Loyalist stock), had considered that she had made a good match because Henry Gifford was an established farmer who had beautiful horses. Together, they had ten children, not all of whom survived infancy. Most were daughters, so when my father entered this world (1885), one of the younger of the ten, he was special, especially in his mother's eyes. My grandfather, Henry Gifford, is supposed to have remarked that if a couple knew the responsibility of raising children, they would not have any. Obviously, he did not heed his own counsel. A discussion between Grandfather Gifford and his brother, some time in the mid-eighteen hundreds, illustrates the difference in values then and a hundred years later: the brothers tried to resolve the issue of whether it was more sinful to work cleaning the barn on Sunday, or to leave the animals standing in filth. I don't know which argument prevailed.

My father's eldest brother, Elias, took up residence in the United States, where he married well in Boston. Like my father, he was a handsome man and, like Aunt Hat, he had an appreciation of fine horses. He had proven himself a crack marksman; I understand that one of the large gun manufacturers engaged him to test their product. I never met him, but I wish I had.

A younger brother, Avard, enlisted in the Great War, served in Europe, was gassed, returned to Canada, and died of the deadly Spanish Flu in 1918, in Vancouver. My father did not enlist; he was busy growing grain for the Allies.

Aunt Hat's sister, Nell, had bad luck with husbands: her first joined the trek to the Yukon during the Gold Rush and was not heard from again. Her second was working on the docks in Halifax when the munitions ship there blew up. He, too, was a casualty. Aunt Nell bore the marks of the disaster as well, one of her eyes thereafter looked in the wrong direction. She was not alone, she said. Outside a hospital door she had seen a ten-pound lard pail filled with nothing but eyes!

Another of my father's sisters who visited us on the farm was Eva, tall and beautiful, a lady through and through. Her married name was Steeves.

Shortly after Aunt Hat established her homestead, she went to California to visit her sister Orlo, the youngest of the family, and reputedly the prettiest of all.

Orlo had been married at eighteen to a druggist, whose last name was Mackay. They had a son, but the marriage faltered and when Aunt Hat visited her in 1914, Orlo was living the life of a single mother. Having a nine year old son curtailed her social life, so when Aunt Hat returned to her acreage in Saskatchewan, she brought her nephew, Wallace Mackay, with her. He never returned to live with his mother. Aunt Hat was genuinely fond of the boy, but she was not a maternal person. Wallace would make the trek over to visit his Aunt Bell, my mother, and she always welcomed him. Aunt Hat had little compunction about working Wallace, but if he ever had any resentment about his fate, he gave no indication.

Aunt Hat had good land which she tilled intelligently, doing most of the work herself with horses. Naturally, she was looked upon as a female aberration: she did not wear skirts, she wore breeches. She did not wear her hair the accepted length, she had it cut almost as short as a man's; she smoked cigarettes when only 'fast' women smoked. In her breeches, leather jacket and old fedora, she could have been mistaken for a man. She did not care.

Our prairie community gossiped, as all self-contained communities do. Gossip was probably aggravated by a lack of outside interests: no television, no radio, many did not subscribe to newspapers or magazines, and some did not even have a telephone. So gossip was the mainstay of communication. As the prairie area in which I grew up had been settled largely by straight-laced, God-fearing, righteous, no-nonsense people, most from Eastern Canada, the British Isles and Western Europe, any deviation from what they looked upon as normal, was viewed with intolerance. Poor Aunt Hat: she was out-of-place, out-of-time, and fine food for the gossip mill. I am sure many looked upon her as a lesbian, but her two marriages, though unsuccessful, should have dispelled that idea. I was too young to be a party to that sort of gossip, and certainly had no idea of the connotations of the word lesbian. My mother had given Jean and I a book to read, 'What Every Young Girl Should Know', which was as innocuous as its title. It generated no inquiries and our mother, probably relieved, vouchsafed no information. I recall being up by the barn when my father opened the gate of the bull's corral to admit a cow in heat. I was startled by his exhortations to me to "Get back, get back," and I did not realize until some time after that it was not my safety he was concerned about, but my loss of innocence.

Aunt Hat kept a pack of hounds for protection and also for coyote control. She liked her hounds, but I did not; they scared me, especially on that day in the late fall when I went on horseback to look for the cows. Near a slough, far from our house, I came upon slaughterhouse entrails deposited there from some farmer's butchering. The skittish horse I was riding (bareback) stopped short at the sight and smells. I almost went over its head. It was a good thing I didn't because Aunt Hat's pack of hounds were devouring their just-discovered feast, snarling and slashing jealously and greed-ily over the choicest portions. They were in no mood for an intruder; the horse, sensing this, broke into a full gallop away. I prayed I would not fall off... my prayers were answered. The incident made me more wary than ever of the hated hounds. Aunt Hat could have them!

One fall the crops had produced well and the price was not bad so Aunt Hat visited California again, dressed like a lady. She trav-elled by rail, via Vancouver and returned to her farm a married woman. Her new husband was a concert pianist who had immi-grated to the United States from Australia, His name: Francis Ashton, Uncle Frank. I don't know what he thought he would be getting into, but I am sure he was dismayed when he found himself marooned on the Saskatchewan prairie. However, he found a sympathetic friend, my mother. She listened while he discussed one of his favorite subjects, horse racing, though it would have been totally foreign to her. I recall one day his telling her that he would like to place a bet on a horse called Silver because a dream the night before had silver in it.

Uncle Frank never worked on the land; that was still Aunt Hat's domain, but he was the original house husband, at least original in our part of the world. The unconventional life style removed Aunt Hat even farther from social acceptance. What decent woman would let her husband do the cooking and housework while she worked on the land with horses? I did not get to know Uncle Frank very well; he did not stay a house husband very long, which was understandable. California beckoned.

I think Aunt Hat favoured me, at least she encouraged any talent I displayed. At that time, *Liberty Magazine* ran Short, Short Story contests. The money was certainly tempting. I wrote a Short Short and proudly showed it to my father. He read it, handed it back and said, "It doesn't mean anything to me." I was deflated by his curt judgment, but I didn't tell Aunt Hat what my father had said when, later, I handed it to her. She did not applaud it, but said, "You've made a fine effort, Ina, keep it up." I did not submit it to the magazine; my father's casual critique was a deterrent, but much later I followed Aunt Hat's injunction to "Keep it up."

In 1928, Aunt Hat had an auction sale, rented the land, and moved to Saskatoon where she lived like a lady and made a home for Wally and Grandma. Wally married and Grandma died in 1938, age 92. Aunt Hat did not marry again, but she still involved herself with horses, 'playing the ponies.'

After my father sold the farm in 1938, he lived in Saskatoon with Aunt Hat for a while, but it was a relationship doomed to failure as it probably had been from the very beginning when she saw him as an infant in his cradle. She was fifteen then and all their lives he resented her big sister attitude as she tried to direct his life.

Aunt Hat's relationship with my mother was one of restrained respect, and, as far as the Elder family went, they never acknowledged any relationship to her if it could be avoided. I think my siblings and I were lucky to have two branches of the family so different; it put spice in our lives.

Four Giffords are buried in the same plot, #156, in the cemetery in Saskatoon; Grandpa died in 1910, age 84; Grandma in 1938, age 92; Aunt Hat in 1958, age 88, and my father in 1959, age 74.

When Wally and I placed an order for a flat black marble grave marker for #156, I said to him, "Isn't it interesting that, after a lifetime of bickering, Dad and Aunt Hat share the same double grave." Wally knew that, once again, irony had gotten the best of my tongue. He said, "Now, Ina" but we shared a smile.

In retrospect, I think that Aunt Hat's character could be summarized in the advice she once gave me, "Ina, when you travel, always go First Class."

Aunt Hat was a First Class person.

The Drowning

I'd been sent over to Aunt Hat's house to comb Grandma Gifford's hair. I didn't want to go, but my mother said that Aunt Hat had to go into town and she didn't want to leave Grandma alone for that long and besides, Grandma liked me to comb her hair. I didn't like doing it; Grandma's long, white hair hung away down her back, my arms soon got tired and besides, her hair smelled funny. No matter how long I combed it, she always wanted me to comb it, "just a wee bit more." I didn't know why it always had to be me, why couldn't Jean do it sometimes? But they said Grandma liked the way I did it. Jean always seemed to get out of everything she didn't want to do.

As soon as Aunt Hat and Uncle Frank came back, I knew I could go home. I hoped they wouldn't be too long. Finally, they came and I was free. As I hurried down the long hill toward home, I saw my mother out in the corn patch. Hurray! Maybe that meant we would have corn-on-the-cob for supper. I loved corn-on-the-cob, especially with lots of butter. My dad loved it, too. My dad put salt on his, but I thought that salt spoiled the taste.

I ran into the house. Jean was in the big chair, reading. I took off my good shoes, put on my runners and hurried out to watch my mother as she opened the husks a peek to see if they were ready. My mother asked about Grandma and I said she was fine. She told

me to go and change into my old jeans because she had a job for me
to do. That made me cross: I had just finished a job. I asked if Jean
couldn't do it, and besides where were the others? My mother just
said it was my job and to hurry. I went, but I didn't hurry. My mother
would be there quite a while, finding the right cobs of new corn.

I went into the house and changed into my old jeans. Jean didn't
look up from her reading. I asked her if she knew what job I had
to do, and where the others were, but she just shook her head. I
was hungry, so I cut myself a thick slice of warm bread and spread
it with lots of butter and jam. Then I hurried out to look at the
kittens. They were Nancy's kittens. Nancy was my very own cat.
Nancy and Daffy were both my cats. I didn't know if Daffy was the
father of the kittens, but I didn't think he was because one of the
kittens was black and Daffy was pure striped orange. Nancy was
what they called a calico. The little black kitten was my very
favourite; he had the cutest white spot by his nose. It would show
up more when he grew up.

I hurried because my mother might wonder where I was; she had
told me to hurry. I didn't want her to find the kittens, they were
our secret, Nancy's and mine. It was the first time she had had
them under the big, red granary, and I wondered why she hadn't
thought of that place before. It was a simply perfect place to hide
kittens, especially from Daffy, who would kill them if they weren't
his, just like male lions did. I had read that in a book. Usually
Nancy had them in the loft, where just anybody could find them
if they cried. Out under the granary, maybe they'd have a chance
to get bigger. Hardly anyone went to the granary in the summer.

A shiver of anticipation went through me, right to my toes, when
I thought of the kittens, so warm and soft, with fur like silk, and
their smell; I just loved the smell of wee kittens. When I buried
my nose in the fur on their necks, they mewed just a little because
they didn't know yet that I really, really loved them and wouldn't
hurt them for anything. Nancy knew I loved them, and she would
purr. Nancy really knew how to purr.

I had never heard any of her kittens purr; they never got big
enough. My mother said kittens had to be drowned before their
eyes opened. Two weeks, that's all it took, two weeks for their eyes
to open. These had been born under the granary eight days ago,
just six more days to go. I began to run toward the granary, but
carefully, so my mother would not see me.

Our granary was different from most granaries. It was a long building, divided into three. It was built on a cement foundation that was open on the south end. A big person couldn't crawl under it, but the hens and Nancy and I could. I was just nine-and-a-half, and skinny. That's how I had found the kittens. I was hunting for eggs and my mother said to check for broody hens that might try to nest under the granary.

Nancy had had her kittens on some rags and an old gunny sack. She was licking them clean when I found her and she took a minute off to purr. I tucked the rags close around the little family to keep them safe and warm. There were four kittens and I noticed the black one right away. It seemed strange to see Nancy with an all-black kitten. I knew it would be my favourite.

When I got to the south end of the granary, I went down on my stomach and wriggled my way toward the back to where the dirt was cooler in the dark. I felt for the kittens because my eyes weren't like Nancy's, they weren't too good in the dark. The kittens weren't where I thought they should be. I felt around for the gunny sack, but there was nothing but dirt. I called Nancy's name, softly, but there was no answer. Nothing stirred, not even a hen. I could see better now, and I crawled this way and that, bruising my knees on pebbles and bits of dried clay. There was nothing. Then I saw it; against the inside of the front of the cement wall, tumbled and torn, the old gunny sack. I knew then: it wasn't a home any more, just a dirty old sack.

I crawled out and blinked in the bright sunlight. When I stood up, I saw what I should have seen before, the marks of the garden rake that had been used to pull the gunny sack out. I wiped the marks away with my foot. I couldn't cry, my whole body was filled with such yearning, to stroke the silky fur, to kiss the little heads, to smell their necks, their clean little-kitten smell. I thought I was going to be sick, right there by the granary.

My mother had pulled enough corn and was starting to shuck it. I didn't say anything, just stood off at a little distance. She said, without looking up, "The pail's in the woodshed." I asked what pail, and she said, "With the kittens." I recoiled as though she had slapped me. "No!" Still she didn't look up. "They were your kittens." But she was the one who drowned them. Let her dump them out, not me. I stood waiting, still seeing the marks of the hated rake. I turned to leave; but then I couldn't. I could not abandon them now. She was right, they were mine and I would do it for them; I'd bury them myself, the right way.

I went to the barn for the pitchfork, and then to the woodshed, where I picked up the pail; it had a lid on it. It was heavy; with the cover on it, it looked like any other pail. I wondered where Nancy was, and if she knew that her kittens were gone. But of course she would; Nancy was a good mother, the very best mother, not like mine. I carried the heavy pail slowly and carefully, so it wouldn't knock against my leg and splash, or make the lid fall off.

I knew where to go, around the corner of the henhouse and down to the manure pile by the small slough. And I knew just where they should be buried, in the warm straw, and deep, so they would be safe from animals. I found the right spot, and then shoved the fork sharply into the yellow straw. When the hole was ready, I put the pail on the very edge and pushed gently. The lid fell off, then the kittens slid onto the lid and then the water washed them into the straw. It was awful.

The little black one – I hadn't named him yet – had fallen out furthest from me; he was dead like the rest. I stood and stared at his tiny, bloated body, and noted with a special kind of horror that the water had made the fur on his back break into waves, as though Nancy had just washed him. I lifted a forkful of straw and threw it on quickly . . . Nancy was coming. But I was too late, the black one wasn't covered. She went right to it and nudged its little wet body with her nose, maybe hoping that it would still be alive. She meowed a plaintive lament, and then came over to me, wanting comfort. I bent and hugged her tight before I took up the fork and finished the hated job.

I put the fork and the pail away in the barn, and then walked slowly down the path toward the house. My mother called and I went over to the corn patch reluctantly. I could still see them so plainly, the little waves in the black kitten's fur.

My mother gestured toward the pile of corn husks and told me to take them to the pigs. I stooped stiffly and gathered an armful.

"Won't Daddy be surprised?" she said. She waited for my answer. "He likes corn," I said dutifully. She laid her hand on my shoulder, but I shrugged it away. "No," she said, "Won't he be surprised that you've grown big enough to dump the kittens?"

The Wind

The thing I remember most about the wind is the sound of it, an other-world sound, not so much threatening as heralding evil; and evil we did suffer from it. It began almost gently, in 1930, and increased its tempo in 1931, the year my mother died in October. She had just a taste of what we had to endure right through to 1937. My mother tried to block the penetrating dust by stuffing wet cloths into vulnerable places, such as around the windows. But the air was so laden with the obnoxious grey substance, it seemed, as in the words of Lewis Carroll:

> "If forty maids with forty mops
> Swept it for half a year,
> Do you suppose, the Walrus said,
> That they could get it clear?"

Sometimes I almost think it was a mercy that she died when she did. At least she was spared the desecration of all for which she had worked so hard. I speculate how she would have coped, she who was so good at coping! In the beginning, the prairies had an even disbursement of rich soil, but the wind changed that; it blew the fine soil from the tops of the hills and knolls, right down to the hard-pan. The wealth of topsoil was gone forever.

The heavy winter snows, that had provided enough subsoil moisture to sustain crops through dry spells, deserted the prairies. That fact was probably the basis for the drought disaster. Our family was among the most severely wounded. My father made a futile effort to scatter manure on the land nearest our house to at least try to keep dust down. It was a case of too little much too late. He had, a few years earlier, abandoned the common practice of turning the stubble under, or burning it, and had purchased an expensive, heavy piece of equipment called a disc plow. The large discs did the work that had been done by the mold boards of the common plow. The disc plow could also be converted to a seeder, so he "killed two birds with one stone," as he plowed the previous year's stubble and seeded the spring crop all at one time. The use of the disc plow probably saved the soil from severe initial erosion, but the cruel winds refused to let the land lie. First the top soil on the knolls gave away, filling the high skies with a greyness that became almost a fixture. The soil drifted on the surface, just as the snows had once done in winter. As the sered tumbling weed and Russian thistle blew into fences and other obstructions, the moving soil was arrested and piled higher and higher, until in some cases it was three times as deep as the fence corners that had originally impeded it.

The reason such erosion could happen went back many years. The original prairie soil was decomposed fibre, an accumulation of centuries of plant growth. The land that in the dirty thirties was reduced to dust, was geologically older than that of the Nile. It took but one generation to destroy it. The results of greed and ignorance taught a lesson in soil management that has changed farming in western Canada. In the post-drought era, farmers attempted to compensate for the loss of the rich top soil by the use of chemicals.

As Ralph Waldo Emerson said, "Society never advances, what it gains on the one hand it sacrifices on the other." Chemicals increased the yield, reduced the incursion of weeds, killed off most of the gophers, but it could not replace the soil the pioneers desecrated.

The government made a half-hearted effort to prevent erosion; it provided carragana hedges for those who wanted them. Carragan sucked up moisture but it could act as a windbreak in the wide, vulnerable fields.

With the air saturated with dirt, the only time a housewife could hazard a clean wash was between two and three o'clock in the morning, when the winds sometimes subsided. Water, of course, was at a premium. Reliable wells dried up; because of the sparse snow, sloughs did not fill. Even the one lake within our driving range by horse and buggy, receded until it, too, was dry. Our main well, 36 feet deep, gave us good, clear water, but the volume declined and there was fear that it would give up the ghost. Without water, there was virtually no garden. The potatoes were puny; staples such as turnips, carrots and beets, and other root crops, were scarcely worth pulling. With the feed supply for animals almost non-existent, the skinny creatures became subject to disease. We lived in a state of disharmony with a Nature that had betrayed us, year after hollow year.

Many farmers packed up what little they had and moved. Those who left our area of north-central Saskatchewan, looked toward northern Alberta for salvation from penury. The Peace River Country seemed to be the Mecca. Even before my mother died, she and my father had discussed moving, weighing the pluses and minuses of the areas where they could establish a new life. Had my mother survived, we, too, might have joined the trek.

One late spring day when I was walking to school, I met a farm family, strangers, who were on the move, They were trying to negotiate a long hill. The emaciated horses were having a hard time trying to pull the old hayrack that was piled high with household goods. I wondered why they were struggling so hard until I approached the back of the hayrack. Then I saw why, the cow had collapsed from exhaustion; she was lying on her side behind the hayrack and was being dragged along the rutted prairie trail. I have never forgotten that pitiful sight.

Model T cars were converted into horse-drawn vehicles dubbed "Bennett Buggies", named for the Canadian Prime Minister of the day, R.B. Bennett, a wealthy lawyer from Calgary. Naturally, he was vilified. My father wrote to him, after our mother's death, outlining the desperate circumstance we were in. A reply eventually came from the Prime Minister's office, but it was a mere form letter that made no reference to my father's subject.

Mr. Bennett was a Conservative, my father a Liberal, which probably had no bearing on the callous reply, but who is to say?

After I left the farm, in the spring of 1935, to seek a better life in the city of Saskatoon, my younger sister, Lois, age 16, soldiered on. My father gave up completely and ended up, at his instigation, in the Mental Hospital in North Battleford. I was not at home to witness the final deterioration of our family. The bank foreclosed in 1938 and my father, who was back home, had an auction sale of the remnants of a lifetime of trying. I was not there for the sale, nor did I want to be. My sister Eva (Petey) was by then in charge and at age eighteen, was ready to join the exodus. My brothers, age sixteen and fourteen, were left to their own devices. What happened to them is another story.

During our years of travail, of swirling dust and lack of water, personal cleanliness was a challenge. The only water we had from the well was hard water, so soap curdled in it, and we had no such luxury as cleansing cream. I am amazed that we came through the ravages of the dust years without any lasting impairment. The major impairment was to our psyches; we were a humbled people who felt we did not deserve a better way of life. But not everyone was an economic victim; there are always those who manage to turn tragedy to their advantage. Farmers who had prospered in the good years, now took advantage of their neighbours' plight. Land became a bargain and those who could afford to, took advantage of the opportunity. If they did not, others would. It was ever thus!

My father was a conscientious farmer, but he had two big strikes against him; too many daughters, and not enough land. He always farmed with horses, while other farmers were converting to the mechanized method of farming. When he first homesteaded his land, my father had used, or rather had tried using a steam engine to pull the machinery. It was a straw-burner, and not suitable to our land for the simple reason that it did not generate enough power to negotiate our rolling hills. I have a photograph of it, an unwieldy piece of equipment. So he stuck with his horses on his half-section of land. Some years he rented other quarters, but the quality of the land for rent did not justify the work he had to put into it.

It did not help that he had two local brothers-in-law who not only had superior land, but had remained bachelors with no others to support but themselves. They prospered, while my father seemed to fall farther and farther behind without even the support of strong sons. The drought marked the end of all hope, that and the fact that my mother was not there to buoy him up. Our life as a family became a classic prairie tragedy.

I realize that wind is essential to the well-being of our planet. In the place where I now live, it takes the foul air that is common to big cities and disperses the acrid fumes that pollute our lungs. Without the wind, we would find large cities uninhabitable. But I don't like to feel wind, or hear it. The menacing sound the wind makes reminds me of the winds that laid waste to my beloved birth-soil. Another after-effect of the drought – I never, ever complain about rain!

 Trails

When our father bought his Model T in 1916, the year I was born, his only direction to the dealer who was bringing it out to the farm from Harris, Saskatchewan, was to "Pick a good one." I don't know if ours was a good one, but I do recall the difficulty it had trying to negotiate the hills on our country trails. Trails, with deep, rutted tracks were standard. The word 'road' did not grace the routes that the Model T Ford was asked to traverse. The hills were steep because no attempt at levelling had been made. Many a time the children had to pile out of the Model T to get behind and shove. Child power was added to horsepower in order to conquer steep hills.

As the horsepower of the cars, and their numbers, increased, the ease of travelling the roads became more important. Municipalities gave tax allowances for a farmer's manual work building roads. It was communal work for summertime. Horses were hitched to graders and fresnels; it was hard, hot work for both man and beast. Little did the animals know that they were working themselves into oblivion. Long handles extending from the back of the fresnels would be used to determine the size of the bite that was taken from the top of a hill. The road was graded wide enough to allow vehicles to pass, and where necessary, hollows would be elevated, thus utilizing the fill that had been taken from the top of the hill. The final result was the luxury of a smooth, wide road where children did not have to get out and push. The roads constructed by man and horse were fine while they were dry. A wet spell played havoc with the newly moved clay; ruts formed, dried rock-hard, and required constant repair. Gravel, in our district, was simply not available.

The evolution of trail to road had a negative side: it removed a source of revenue that many farmers enjoyed. The rudimentary trails had followed straight lines, up and down, with rarely a diversion. This meant that they went through small sloughs and low spots that retained water after the spring melt or a heavy rain: mudholes formed; the humble Model T could not cope. When the cars became bogged down, the closest neighbour's horses would be pressed into service to pull out the hapless car. Farmers living near a mudhole counted on being reimbursed for the use of their horses and their time. Some farmers were even suspected of replenishing the waters that kept the mudhole a money-pit for them!

As with most prairie children, we did not learn how to swim; not enough water, not enough time. Few of our parents could swim and there was no concern that we did not know how. We loved to paddle in the sloughs that held their water. As the sloughs slowly dried, we enjoyed the company of huge black-shelled water beetles and we endured the itch imposed upon us by a mysterious water insect or parasite. The itch was looked upon as part of the experience of a slough bath. In a health class in school, the teacher asked a farm lad how often he took a bath and was given the nonchalant reply, "When there's water in the slough."

My sister, Lois, said to me not long ago that there were three things she regretted she did not learn: how to type, how to swim and how to sing. I did not learn how to swim until we came to Toronto. Swimming lessons were given at a collegiate near us and I determined that I would learn, even though I was sure I would be the oldest and the fattest; I was relieved to find I was not either one. But I did discover that I was a natural floater; I simply lay down on my back in the water and I was buoyant as a cork.

When I was a child, the First of July picnic was the big holiday event of our summer. It was held at Crystal Beach, a lake two miles from the town of Harris, Saskatchewan. As Harris was sixteen miles from our farm, it was quite a pilgrimage to get there. Our Model T would line up beside all the other Model Ts in the picnic grounds. We would eat our picnic on our patch of grass by the car, indifferent to the fact that we were trampling Saskatchewan's flower, the tiger lily, now protected as it almost became extinct during the dry 30s. On one occasion, probably a Royal anniversary, we were each given 25 cents by the teacher to spend as we pleased.

Oh, joy! The big wooden pavilion that housed the concession area (and the dance floor), was a magnet for a child with twenty-five whole cents to spend. I patrolled up and down trying to decide which I wanted: ice cream, candy, chocolate bars, such an array of enticements. I finally made up my mind: I bought an orange; an orange was the ultimate in extravagance.

There were all kinds of races, the three-legged and the potato-sack being my favourites. There were fierce baseball rivalries. It was a time of great baseball on the prairies; teams entered from near and far bringing their reputations and prestige. I don't think much money changed hands, at least there was no admission charge.

No wonder we looked forward to July 1st all year. If the weather was thoughtless enough not to cooperate, there was no tomorrow to compensate for the lovely, lost day. It was July 1st or nothing.

My father did not like to go to the picnic at Crystal Beach unless there was a name politician who would address the crowd from the outdoor platform. A speaker with good voice projection had the advantage, as there was no such thing as an amplifier.

I have a vivid memory of my mother sitting by the lakeside with other mothers as they kept a sharp eye on their many offspring, a family of six being normal. While shyness was not one of my attributes, in this particular memory, I am huddling up against her and she is coaxing me to try wading in the lake. I was afraid of the waves.

Winter travel on the prairies was by sleigh, usually a grain box from the wagon transferred to runners. The more affluent owned a cutter which had slim, curved runners, an upholstered seat for two, a curved dashboard, often ornamented. The fine, well bred horse, or team, had fine harness with bells. A buffalo robe, lined with plaid wool, was de rigueur.

When comfort was the prime need, many farmers built their own winter travel outfits. It would be on runners, completely enclosed by white canvas. Inside there would be a small coal-burning stove which advertised its presence by a tall chimney that extended above the roof of the rig. They appeared to be top-heavy, but I never heard of one upsetting in spite of the often-hazardous trails.

A winter sleigh disaster did happen to a young neighbour. He was hauling a sleigh load of pigs into market for his uncles. It was late winter and the trails had become rutted and slippery. On the side of a hill, the sleighful of pigs began to tip dangerously and the animals were all thrown to that side. The young man stopped the horses and got out to see if he could prop the sleigh to prevent it from going right over. But it was to no avail; the sleigh fell with him under it. The horses stood as they had been commanded, while he smothered to death in the snow. There was an added poignancy to the tragedy; his family learned of his death when it was broadcast over the radio.

After a long, cold winter, the early days of spring were greeted with joy. On a mild day, young people would set off for a joyous sleigh ride, perhaps their last for that winter. Then, without warning, a raging blizzard could hit. Blizzards, combined with plunging temperatures, are killers. On this spring day, the group of young people had not dressed warmly and the blinding blizzard caught them totally by surprise. They swiftly unhitched the horses, turned the sleigh box upside down and huddled under it while the elements raged. The horses finally made their way to their barn and thus alerted the family at home that there was trouble; they had no recourse but to wait out the storm and pray. Fortunately, no lives were lost, but it was a narrow escape.

The fact that our social life was localized, in both winter and summer, could be attributed to the limitations of our means of transport. There was a limit to the distance a horse and rig could travel in one day. The townsites along the railroads were determined by the speed and endurance of the horse. As motorized vehicles became the norm, many towns became redundant and withered away. Then as single farms were incorporated into farms of monolithic proportions, more business than farms, with no animals, the transportation of the grain output required large-capacity vehicles that could travel long distances. The common grain elevator, landmark of the prairies for so long was doomed. Huge trucks hauled huge volumes of grain to huge depots that were built to handle varied crops. Recently, the value of wheat in Saskatchewan was exceeded, for the first time, by that of another crop, canola. Canola is favored world wide as a source of superior cooking oil. Railroads that had been the lifeline of lively communities were closed and the tracks torn up. Families drifted to the cities; the pattern of living was altered on the prairies forever, all in the name of progress.

The day that my father ordered his Model T and told the dealer to send him "a good one," was a watershed. But, like most watersheds in our lives, how could he know? But the horses knew! They shied at the sight of their rival, the motor car, causing many a spill.

 Porky

Every spring my father would buy two young pigs from a neighbour and they would be slaughtered in the fall after the snow was on the ground and the meat could be frozen.

The children were expected to help with the slaughter, hold the pig down while our father wielded the sharpened knife. The pig would then be allowed to get on its feet where the blood oozed onto the snow until the animal collapsed. The slaughtering was part of farm life; what I didn't like was being served the liver that same night for supper. I simply could not eat it and was accused of being overly sensitive.

Early one spring, when I was nine I think, my father told me to come with him to help get the new pigs. We took the wagon, a bumpy ride because all the frost had not yet left the ground. When we got to the farm my father chose the two pigs he wanted as I leaned over the pigpen fence watching.

Then I saw something I simply had to have; the smallest, tiniest, cutest pig so little it didn't look real. The runt. My neighbour laughed when I exclaimed over it and said I could have it if I could catch it. What a foolish thing to do! But I was over the fence like a flash, scooped up the squealing little pig and was back again before the charging sow could defend it. On the way home, I cuddled the little thing inside my coat to keep it warm. He was so small I could stand him on my two hands. I called him Porky, he was black with a band of white around his middle, just like a real pig.

My mother was not too pleased to see him. She knew, in spite of my promises, who would have to raise the delicate little animal: my mother. Porky was put in a wooden box-pen in the corner of the kitchen and through her diligence and patience, he survived.

I played with Porky as if he were a doll, dressing him in doll clothes and covering him with little blankets all his own. When the weather improved he would lie by the house outside the kitchen door snuggled up with my big cat, Daffy, who didn't mind providing companionship and warmth. Daffy was not in the house; my mother didn't like cats in the house, dogs yes, but not cats.

Then a bad thing started to happen. Porky began to grow. I could still pick him up and cuddle him but he was getting heavier bit by bit.

When July came I was in a dilemma; July was berry picking month. All the older children would drive in the buggy several miles to the sandhills where the saskatoons were in abundance. We took several hundred-pound flour and sugar sacks and lots of lunch and water. We picked berries all day. But what about Porky? He would need to be fed. He had graduated from the kitchen to the henhouse which had been the first barn.

The day's milk had been put through the separator so, before we left for berry picking, I hastily prepared a dish I knew Porky would love; cold boiled potatoes, a few bits of bread, a handful of raisins, a little oatmeal and the whole thing garnished with stolen cream. Porky would love it, I knew. I didn't show it to anyone, just tiptoed out and put it by his straw bed in the corner of the henhouse.

It was getting dark when we got home with our load of berries. My mother told me to go and shut the henhouse door so the hens couldn't get out until we opened it in the morning. We had to keep them safe from the coyotes who would sneak up and kill just for the fun of it if the poultry were out early. It was scarey going out in the late evening dusk all by myself. The inside of the henhouse was dark and Porky would be asleep. I decided to tiptoe in and give him a pat so he would know I was back. I went in and he was there asleep on his straw. I bent over and patted him but he didn't respond. I patted him harder and discovered to my horror that he wasn't warm; Porky was dead. He had eaten every bit of his dish I had so lovingly prepared. I'd killed Porky with kindness.

We buried little Porky the next day in a grave on the top of the knoll west of the house. I made a little wooden cross and cried and cried. My mother gave me a rare hug and her words of comfort and wisdom, "There's one good thing" she said, as if in relief, "Now he will never have to be a patch of red on the snow."

 # Pets

Pets are an integral part of most children's lives, especially on the farm. I have devoted a whole chapter to my little pig, Porky, who was very special. Daffy, my very own cat, was special, too; he was the one who kept Porky warm when Porky was a small piglet.

Daffy was a big cat, very handsome, with burnt orange tabby stripes. We had raised him from a kitten and I cannot remember how and why he became Ina's cat, but he did. He went with me everywhere outside (my mother didn't allow cats in the house). When I went to feed the hens, he would be riding on my shoulder, his favorite perch. He followed me as I did my chores, whether it was bringing in the coal or getting water from the well. Of course we talked and even to this day as I pass the neighbours' houses on my daily walk, I talk to the cats on the doorstep or windowsill in their own cat parlance and they talk back.

Anything Daffy demanded was alright with me, but on one occasion it got me into trouble with my mother. That fall she had ordered a heavy tweed winter coat for me from the catalogue. It had an interlining of leather and the heather-coloured tweed was good quality. I wore it proudly, until one day I came in from feeding the hens. My mother looked at me and said, "What is wrong with your new coat?" I didn't know what she meant. Then she showed me, the whole length of the coat on the right side was shredded. I hadn't noticed it before. Right away I knew the culprit: when Daffy rode on my shoulder he got there by climbing up the front of my coat; he preferred the right side. His sharp claws had caught in the tweed and had broken the threads all the way down the front. My mother ordered the shoulder-riding to stop at once unless I picked him up and put him there. Oh well, he was getting pretty heavy for my child-shoulder anyway. My penalty was having to wear a shredded coat for the rest of the winter. Daffy didn't take kindly to his rejection and would follow me with plaintive meows, his tail twitching in rebellion.

I always preferred cats to dogs. Actually, I was afraid of dogs, the large ones anyway. But our dogs were small; it started with Tiny, who was just that. I don't know where or how my father obtained her, but our introduction to Tiny was as she lay on top of a pile of empty mail bags and snarled at anyone who approached her. Not an auspicious start.

Tiny was a beautiful little terrier, obviously well bred. Her head was particularly dainty and her coat distinctive with large patches of color: black, white and tan. She was widely admired. She soon became reconciled to the fact that she was part of our family, and that our father was her special protector. Tiny liked to follow him to the field. When he was plowing she took special pride in catching any gopher reckless enough to come her way. She had a neat trick of disposing of the gopher, which seemed to be almost her size. She would grab it by the back of the neck and toss it into the air: by the time it landed, it was dead; she had broken its neck. Then she would neatly dispose of her victim by putting it in the newly turned furrow where it would be buried the next time the plow made its round. My father said she was worth her weight in gold. The neighbours thought so too, as there was always a waiting list for her next pups. She had one litter a year, sired by a black and white terrier a bit bigger than she was; in her younger years she would have a litter of three or four, but in the later years she had only one pup a year.

We kept a neat little black and white one for ourselves. My brother, John, a toddler was just old enough to put his own spin on words so instead of puppy he said pooey, so Pooey it was. Pooey was born accident prone, or so it seemed. His first bad accident was when he tried to get out from under the warm kitchen stove. As a pup it had been no problem, but Pooey grew bigger and stouter so getting out from under the stove required lying on his side and pulling himself arduously, a manoeuvre that took some time. This particular day he was part way out when the big kettle on the top of the stove boiled over, spilling scalding water onto his neck. The poor dog, it didn't kill him and he finally recovered but the hair never grew in again, and Pooey never again went under the stove.

Pooey's next accident happened when my father was harvesting. Pooey had wandered into the tall grain in front of the horse-drawn binder and before my father realized the dog was in peril, the sharp binder knife had severed the cord at the back of his back leg . . . it was completely cut through. My mother tried to keep bandages on it, but Pooey would remove them with his teeth every time. He hobbled about on three legs, as we anticipated he would do for the rest of his life. But a miracle happened. I don't know how long it took, but the two severed ends, which had been a good inch apart, mended together; perhaps his licking the wound had done it. I still can't believe that leg of Pooey's was completely restored.

We didn't have sheep, just lambs. A crusty old Scottish neighbour had a large flock of sheep, the ones with the gentle-looking black heads. His son, Johnny, and I were firm friends and every spring I would be presented with an orphan lamb. Usually it was an orphan because the ewe had given birth to three and she could only suckle two. I got the spare. My poor mother would be the one who cared for the wee orphan until it could function on its own. It would be kept in a warm box in the kitchen and she would feed it from a nippled bottle on demand. My mother must have dreaded the arrival of each spring's orphan lamb. We got a call from Johnny's father the year I was ten that they had a spare lamb. My father and I drove the four miles in our Model T to bring it home. When we got there we found a surprise: since the phone call, the ewe had had another lamb, making an unprecedented four in all. So that spring my mother coped with twin lambs.

The lambs had the run of the barn in the winter and the run of the yard in summer. In the winter they haunted the foot of the stairwell where the feed was thrown down from the loft. In the summer my father would sometimes tether them in a field where they could justify their existence by eating weeds. He had devised the tether with two swivels so they would not be imperilled by the rope. I would worry about them down in the field at night all alone and unprotected from coyotes.

The last lamb I had, I named Nancy. Nancy grew to be a strong-willed sturdy animal. We found we could ride her, no mean feat as staying on top of long wool is not as easy as one would think it should be. In the spring my father clipped her, which made riding much easier.

Late in the spring my mother announced that she had spoken to the butcher and he would take Nancy the next time he came around. By this time, I had seen many lambs come and go. I decided I would play a game with Nancy in the time we had left. I would put a hand on her head, facing her, and then back away. She soon learned to lunge after me. But I had forgotten that Nancy was no longer a lamb. She was now a big, strong sheep and before the butcher's visit it came to the point where we were getting afraid to go out in the yard because Nancy would charge at us. So it was almost a relief to see her go. But the week after she left, when my mother announced that she had a surprise for supper, lamb chops, warm memories flooded back; that night I didn't eat supper.

Health

The word hospital had an ominous connotation when I was young: people did not go to the hospital unless they were dying. The fact that anyone would be cured of a disease there was a remote possibility. It is difficult to imagine that every aspect of doctoring was so primitive in relation to what is available less than a hundred years later.

In the 1920s, a girl in our district died one summer and her death was attributed to the fact that she "had eaten green apples." It was probably appendicitis, at that time not a recognized affliction. Our mother made sure that we did not eat any green apples!

We were a lucky family: no broken bones, even though every time my father cranked the Model T it seemed he invited a broken cranking arm. And I don't know how we escaped disaster at school when we pumped the big swing until the velocity took us up and over the top of it in a full circle. Where was the teacher?

All parents were afraid of diptheria, but we escaped it. The only noxious disease that invaded our home was whooping cough. One long summer, all the children in our family came down with it; I can still hear its distinct sound. There was no mistaking whooping cough, though no doctor was called for a diagnosis.

Dr. George had an office in Harris, sixteen miles away and the closest hospital was in Rosetown, about twenty-five miles from Harris.

I seemed to be plagued with ear trouble; our father had his own home remedies for that: a five pound, cloth bag of salt would be heated in the kitchen stove oven, then the bag placed on the patient's pillow and the aching ear laid on the hard bag of warm salt. It didn't work! Another cure was tobacco smoke, straight from his pipe, blown into the ear. It didn't work! A poultice of boiled onions would be made; it too was supposed to have drawing power. It too didn't work! To be honest, though, something at one time or other may have had drawing power, because I can remember the repulsive, yellow excretion from my ear covering the pillow.

My older sister, Jean, and I were very ill one early spring. I think it was in 1922, when our mother was in the hospital in Saskatoon where she gave birth to our first brother, Ted. Grandma Gifford, who would be seventy-seven then, was keeping house for her son and his family. I don't know what we came down with, but I suspect it was pneumonia. As we would be six and eight at the time, and were deathly ill, I have only a sketchy recollection, just the remembrance of being very sick. My father said he was in despair when, at the height of our fever, he stood over us knowing that the disease could be fatal. He said a voice told him to make the sign of the cross over us, which he did. We recovered, I am not sure over what interval of time, but I remember the first day I was out of bed and in the kitchen: my grandmother gave me a treat, a slice of bread with raspberry jam on it. After I had taken a bite, I could not finish it, it tasted so funny. She was chagrined; I have a vivid recollection of that, her disappointment, and the awful taste of that bread and jam.

There were no cure-alls in our home, such as today's Aspirin. If we had an infection, a bread poultice would be applied. Bealing was a term used for an infected appendage; my mother seemed to be afflicted fairly often with bealing fingers; infection around her finger nails. She never mentioned any pain associated with it, but then, my mother wouldn't. Hang nails are a problem with me; I probably inherited them from my mother.

The word antibiotic had not entered our vocabulary: Raleigh's ointment and liniment sufficed. My father had a favourite cure...actually, it was for the horses: Dr. Bell's it was called, bought from the Watkin's man, who called in the summer at every farm, as did the Raleigh's man, with their assortment of nostrums for man and beast, and wondrous spices for the kitchen.

A few drops of Dr. Bell's was supposed to take care of most every ailment an animal could have. My father reasoned that if it was good enough for a horse, it should be good for children too. It must have tasted awful because we made a big fuss if we had to take only a drop or two. I do not recall that it did much good but, thankfully, it did us no lasting harm.

Every year there would be an infestation of head lice in the school. The district nurse would come, examine us and pronounce us infested. Then our mother would go to work, using the reliable fine-tooth comb. Every evening we would take turns bending our heads over a sheet of paper while our mother combed the lice onto it. Our job was to kill the lice with the back of a thumb nail before they escaped. Nits were another matter, the comb could not dislodge the nits that clung like glue to the strands of hair. The cure for nits was coal oil, soaked in a rag that was drawn across the affected strand of hair. It was a tedious job for mother and child. But eventually the lice episode would be over and we were cautioned, again, to not put on a strange toque. Having lice seemed to be a child's rite of passage and none was more relieved when it was over than our mother's tired arm!

In the very early pioneer days, my grandmother Elder had been the community midwife. Having had six children of her own, she was considered well versed in the skill. That duty, after she resigned from it, was taken over by a neighbour, a much younger woman, one of those people who seemed able to cope with almost anything. Just before I turned eighteen, a neighbour from four miles away, drove over and asked, since his wife was expecting soon, would I come and help until the baby came. It was a first child and a home delivery. It was January, a claustrophobic month on the prairies. I was glad to get out of the house. I don't know why they got me: the expectant mother and I were neophites; I had helped at the birth of animals, as most farm children had, but not at the birth of a human. Not long after I got there, the baby gave indications of coming sooner than anticipated. The father retreated to the barn until I ran, desperately, to tell him to go quickly for the midwife, about five miles away. There was no telephone to alert her that he was coming. So, off he hurried in the sleigh, leaving me alone with a scared mother screaming with pain and pleading for help. I boiled water; I knew that boiling water was a basic requirement for a home delivery. I grasped my neighbour's two hands while she pushed, sweated and cried. I would have cried, too, but that would only have made matters worse. I think that that was the longest time of my life. The baby's head was showing as its father drove, with the midwife, into the yard. It was a girl. They told me, after, that I had "done a good job." Today it would be called 'Keeping my cool.'

When we were growing up, our mother had fingered Jean for a teacher, and she was exceedingly foresighted when she thought I should be a nurse, but a nurse specializing in nutrition. For an era when the word calorie had not yet invaded our thinking, being a nutritionist was advanced, indeed. Teacher, nurse and secretary were the standard occupations deemed proper for proper young ladies. The fact that my first, tentative steps into the business world were taken through the secretarial channel, was because the career of nursing did not appeal to me, probably a direct result of my traumatic experience that January day in 1934.

There were certainly more medications and ointments for the livestock on our farm than there were for people. An interesting episode evolved around a young horse, named Mack, whom my father had raised. When he was half-grown, he suffered an injury on his right foreleg, just above the hoof; his leg had become entangled in barbed wire and, in trying to free himself, he had sawed the leg back and forth, causing severe injury. It healed over in time, with the help of Raleigh's ointment, but the leg did not return to normal. My father would let the horses roam early in the spring, there were no fenced fields to confine them, but they did not stray far. Horses from other farms sometimes joined them as they all enjoyed the freedom of the open fields. Later in the spring, my father would bring his horses in to the stable to ready them for the spring work.

This particular spring, one horse was missing: Mack. Inquiries were made in the district but there was no trace of the bay two year old with the black mane and tail. As every horse was needed, to lose a sturdy young animal was much cause for concern. My father decided to visit some of the neighbours personally, to alert them to his loss. One farmer on whom he called was an elderly man who farmed south of us; he was a crochety character and not too approachable. By this time, work was beginning on the land. When my father drove into this gentleman's farmyard, the horses had been hitched for the afternoon's work, and one of the hitched horses was Mack!

When the elderly farmer was told that the bay two year old was my father's horse, he denied it and claimed that Mack was his own. My father told him he could prove it was his horse: he told the old man to look at the right front leg and that above the hoof there was a disfiguring injury. When the neighbour saw it, he reluctantly relinquished the horse. Mack's injury had paid off!

Animal fat in the diet was not the pariah it is considered to be today. Huge kettles of boiling beef or pork fat provided the delicious doughnuts my mother often made. The schoolteacher who boarded with us, George Lyon, had frequent bouts of heartburn and this called for frequent glasses of water and baking soda. Home remedies were the norm: the baking soda also took care of mosquito and other insect bites.

We had a thick, brown book that was kept, for easy reference, on the kitchen shelf above the flour bin. The Home Encyclopedia (or some such title) was a treasure of advice and information, everything from cooking recipes to pages that were considered unfit for young eyes. Similar big, brown books that encompassed every possible need or emergency, were to be found in almost every pioneer household: they provided a strong psychological benefit.

My mother had poor teeth and while she was still in her thirties, she had them all extracted. Her false teeth were crude by today's standards. When she smiled, she showed a generous portion of her upper gums; her mouth was not well shaped to accommodate dentures. As I look back, now, it was rather endearing. As she would have to make the trip to far-off Saskatoon for any work on her dentures, they were never checked or relined, but she never complained about them.

I had many toothaches, caused by decaying molars. One night I cried with pain almost all night long. The next morning, in frustration, my father took the pliers from his tool chest and, after many false starts, succeeded in pulling the offending tooth, without benefit of pain killer. Apart from a glass of Scotch whisky, there was no painkiller in the house; and Scotch was not to be given to a child, no matter how bad the pain.

We brushed our teeth regularly, our mother saw to that, using salt or the good old standby, baking soda. Saturday night was bath night in the winter: one large, square galvanized tub of water, six children taking turns, smallest first, the water replenished now and again with dippers of warm water from the kitchen stove reservoir. We bathed in the kitchen in front of the cookstove, with water from snow that had been melted. In the summer, we had a larger tub, the slough, which was a great deal more fun. We donned bathing

suits and paddled about in company with huge, black water beetles and myriads of other unidentified fauna that, as the season
wore on and the water receded, gave us the itch. The itch would
be relieved with, what else?, the ubiquitous baking soda.

I suppose it was something of a miracle that none of us ever had
a broken bone, though my brother, Ted, had to go to the hospital in Saskatoon some time after our mother died. I had already
left home, but I understand that his shin bone was 'riddled with
holes' and there was fear that he might lose his leg. Thankfully,
he recovered.

My grandmother Gifford fell and broke her wrist in Saskatoon
when she was eighty. As she then lived alone on the third floor of
a large rooming house, I was sent in from the farm to keep her
company and to give help. It was January, winter holidays, and I
was thoroughly homesick. I relieved my homesickness by writing
letters home. My favourite retreat for this consoling exercise was
the lowered seat in the second-floor bathroom, which I used as a
writing table. I knelt beside it and poured out my yearning heart:
I was nine years old. But I am indebted to Grandma Gifford, she
lived to be ninety two and said she had never had a headache in
her life. Neither have I: thank you for that gene, Grandma G.

I am not sure that our mother's death should fall under the category health. Nothing could save her after she contracted child-
bed fever in the Rosetown hospital when Iris was born, October 23,
1931, our parent's nineteenth wedding anniversary. It was the pre-
penicillin era. At that time a ten-day confinement was normal; she
contracted the virus just before she was to come home and was not
the only mother to do so. When my children were born in the
Saskatoon Hospital in 1943 and 1945, a ten-day stay was still the
norm. Today the pendulum has swung the other way; mothers and
their babies are discharged, almost in hours, sometimes to the
detriment of both. Health care is not an exact science!

Addendum: with two pipe-smokers in residence, the air in our
one-storey house was blue all winter. No cancer . . . perhaps tobacco
was cleaner then.

On the subject of health, I'll let my father have the last word,
he said, "If you have more than four children, there will be something wrong with one of them all the time."

Sewing

Our quality of life altered dramatically after our mother's death in 1931. I sometimes speculate now how she would have handled the Depression morass. Our family without her was like a captain-less vessel, manned by an untrained crew, heading into a tropical storm. Take the matter of clothing.

When we were children, our mother knitted endlessly for us. Now no one knew how to knit! ... that made a basic difference. Even buttons became a crisis. The zipper had not yet entered the scene; buttons were it. But when my two younger brothers lost theirs from their winter coats, there was a mad search for replacement buttons; other garments had to be cannibalized to provide the immediate essentials. It was a small matter, but indicative of the straits we were in. There was no money for anything. The tins of my father's favourite tobacco were rarely depleted but things like shoes and stockings were in short supply indeed. I recall that when my brother, John, a lad of nine at the time, wanted shoes for school we had to cut sections from an old inner tire tube and tie those with string around his feet.

Our father must have written to his sister in the east and her response was to send us a large wooden box of used clothing. I pounced on it with glee. We had a Singer treadle sewing machine which I had not been taught how to use. I soon taught myself.

To this day, I do not cut into a length of new yard goods without a grateful nod to the Gods of Provision; I had spent so many years 'making over'. I shudder now when I think of some of the things I made; one garment in particular, I recall, a dress for Iris when she was about three. It was fashioned from an old garment's navy blue wool and I made it in a style suitable to an adult. The little waif appeared at a community social in my proudly-fashioned creation. She must have looked like a dwarf, but no one said anything; at least they knew I had tried.

The Pandora's Box that came from the city streets in the east were as far removed from suitability to our climate and lifestyle as

they could be ... a black satin coat with a luxurious beige fur col-
lage ... a pale yellow crepe dress that would require a skilled dry
cleaner's tender care ... silk stockings several sizes too small and
boasting a run or two.

I spread the treasures on the clean granary floor and considered
what could be done. I had no patterns, of course, and they would
not have been of much help; it was an extreme case of "Cut your
garment to fit your cloth." Seams had to be ripped endlessly, thread
was in short supply and the luxury of matching thread color to
cloth a fantasy.

Later in life, hundreds and hundreds of garments later, when
my ability as a designer and seamstress received accolades, the
foundation had been laid on that granary floor.

(I digress now: when I visited New York city in 1956 from the
west, I had made myself a wardrobe, largely from drapery material, that included a full-pleated skirt, a blouse and a collar. The
material, draped beautifully, had a western flavour with large wheat
sheaves, bucolic western scenes, all in earth colours. The blouse
was plain brown cotton and I fashioned the separate large, sailor-
style collar to match the skirt with the pattern showing to advantage. I lost count of the number of times both men and women
stopped me, on the street and elsewhere, to ask where I had
obtained the outfit.)

In the heart of the Dirty Thirties in the west, relief trains of
goods and supplies came, mostly from Ontario. I do not have
happy memories of those. The apples we received were strictly
windfall, the turnips large and coarse. When a carload arrived at
the train station, naturally the reeves and other authorities got first
dibs. Our father went down to Valley Centre, seven miles away, and
brought home our share. Wonder of wonders, it included a piece
of yard goods and a little wine coloured wool dress for Iris.

I pounced on the cotton yard goods and made myself a dress.
Eventually, it had to be washed and the washing was a disaster; the
printed material had been little better than cheesecloth and every
trace of the green checked design disappeared forever! The little
wool dress for Iris fared not much better. When I was putting it
on her the wool literally disintegrated in my hands. I wonder how
long it had been in an eastern attic. I know the good people of
Ontario meant well ... but. When I tell young people today that for
five years, between the ages of fifteen and twenty, I and my sisters

had no new item of clothing, they simply cannot comprehend it.

My mother had been thrifty about mending and altering. Once, as I watched her mend a shirt of father's, she commented, "It must be a labour of love, no one in their right mind would do it." She did other sewing for my father! Once she struggled with the huge canvas that carried the cut grain on the binder to be tied into sheaves. It had torn and she attempted to mend it on her faithful Singer. I don't know if she succeeded.

With four girls in a row, she could hardly keep up to our growing and of course there were plenty of innovations and hand-me-downs. I have a picture of myself in a cotton dress she had made, with a wide, contrasting band around the waist which she had inserted to adjust to my height. I was tall for my age and probably merited the nickname, Shorty.

During the war years I got into a different kind of sewing business: I began making stuffed toys. This was wartime and toys that were obtainable were mostly fashioned of wood, heavy and clumsy, even those were scarce. I was fortunate that, through business connections, I could obtain what were known as felted mattresses. I used the mattress filling to stuff cotton toys. The cotton material (also scarce) was supplied to me by the Hudson's Bay Company who in turn took most of my production. I designed the toys and women made them in their homes. During wartime, businesses had to be registered; I was the only Saskatchewan toy manufacturer registered with the Wartime Prices and Trade Board in Ottawa. I was required to submit each new design to them for approval and the sample would be returned to me. In one instance, an original trumpeting elephant was not and, upon inquiry, I was told that it had been donated to a charity. A few years after the war, I saw my elephant trumpeting majestically in a department store window. I had been had!

Later, in the city, I bought my own sewing machine; a Singer portable electric, Model 90, that boasted a curved wooden cover. It cost me $40, secondhand, in 1940. I still use it today, over fifty years later. It has no frills, not even a reverse stitch but it sews beautifully because I coddle it, even doing my own repairs, though, truth to tell, not much repairing has been required. I tell the family they can cremate it with me.

After Henry and I were married and our children were small (a boy and twin girls in less than two years), I started to take in sewing.

A word to all seamstresses: if you are going to do that, do it for fun people.

My fun people were high school girls, a merry clique. Their enthusiasm for clothes knew no bounds. Datelines were always an imperative: "I have to have it for a week from Friday because…" Their seamstress becomes involved with their lives and their loves. Sometimes the love-of-the-moment would wait in the wings while the newest creation was being fitted. For one occasion, a graduation dance, three young lovelies, all size six, wanted special dresses.

I was sworn to secrecy by each who came separately for the fitting. But I was faced with a dreadful dilemma: each of the three had brought me the same pattern and, while the materials were not identical, they were all light blue. What to do? I could not even fudge the scalloped neckline to make them a bit different; even a hint would be tantamount to betrayal. So the three pretty dresses arrived, I hope not simultaneously, at the ball. No one said a thing about it to me; after all, I had kept my part of the bargain.

Most of the people for whom I sewed were friends, or friends of friends. One special friend of mine who had a 'fitting handicap' of being very long-waisted and long-armed, wanted a whole wardrobe to wear on her author/husband's cross-Canada motor trip. Done. Her friend, the wife of a professor, wanted a dress for her daughter. I forget the occasion, but of course it was urgent. I relented, and in spite of more work on hand than I liked to contemplate, said I would make one dress. The professor arrived, on his bicycle, with a suitcase full of material!

As the children got older, I gave up taking in sewing with great relief. Instead, for a time, I made display garments for a friend who owned a yard goods shop. I also designed and made hats and purses from the remnants of materials that had been bought from her business.

Naturally, I sewed everything for our identical twin daughters, even when they enjoyed a brief stint as models in Toronto. I recall one occasion when an affluent suitor called for them, he chided me when he found I had New Democratic Party sympathies. (After all, I was from Saskatchewan!) and he said, "How could you when your daughters are going out in thousand dollar outfits." He didn't know I had made those thousand dollar outfits. We did not tell.

Of all my sewing memories, the one most poignant is the sound of my mother's treadle Singer working late one Christmas Eve. The next morning Jean and I found as our gifts, carefully crafted brown cotton petticoats; the gifts that had been ordered for us had arrived broken, too late to be replaced. I hope we exclaimed over the lovely garments our mother had made, and gave her a kiss. I doubt that we did, children can be very insensitive.

This is my belated recognition of a mother's devotion. But before I leave the subject of sewing, I must pay tribute to dear, old Aunt Annie who was not related to us, but who was known to all the district as Aunt Annie. She had come from England with her sister, Mrs. Tyson who, with a large family, mostly male, had homesteaded north of our farm. Aunt Annie was commandeered to come and take care of our family while our mother was in Saskatoon having a baby. Aunt Annie took her duties seriously, to the extent that she brought a big, white, flour sack of holey long black wool stockings out of a closet and put us to work darning. Our mother had knitted the stockings and she was probably so busy knitting, she did not have time to darn. Darn, we did, my sisters and I. Aunt Annie inspected every darn when it was finished, to make sure it was done right. I put my expertise in darning to good use later, especially in wartime, when darning was a must.

Thank you, Aunt Annie, the darning perfectionist.

Play

My father said that all those children in our not very large house were bearable except in the spring and the fall. In the spring, I suppose, our parents could scarcely wait to get us outside and in the fall the thought of a long winter confined with the noise and confusion (and fighting) of an energetic family was almost too much to bear.

We did not have many toys to play with. Santa was not as generous as he became for our grandchildren. The Eaton catalogue was the source of all desire; we almost wore out its pages but we knew enough not to choose two toys; one per child was the rule. And the possibility that we would get the chosen toy was remote indeed, if our wishes were beyond the family purse; but no one come right out and told us that.

We hung our stockings, long, black, hand-knit by our mother, with our names printed very legibly on a scrap of paper pinned to our personal stocking. Sometime during the night one or two of us would crawl across the bedroom floor and quietly, oh so quietly, feel the closest stocking to see if it miraculously held a treasure. A loud no-nonsense voice would bring us back to reality. The thing we were feeling for in the stocking was an orange, which always held the place of honour in the stocking toe. If the orange was not there, no Santa yet. I don't know how our mother obtained the oranges because they certainly could not be brought back from town by our father; the long trip in the sleigh in a Saskatchewan winter would soon take care of a timid hot climate orange.

One toy I recall vividly, I don't know why. I had probably asked for a doll, Eaton Beauty preferred. What I got was a small china Kewpy-type doll with movable arms. It was only about four inches tall and not the kind to be dressed with much ease or satisfaction. But I loved that doll, she had a sweet face and I would lie in bed clutching her until her china was warm. She was no Eaton Beauty but she was mine. I suppose it was one of the years when the crop had not survived the many hazards it had to endure: frost, rust, cutworm, sawfly, hail, the stinky stinkweed. Oh well, maybe next year would yield an Eaton Beauty crop.

My father did not believe in Christmas gifts and was very unenthusiastic about the Sandy Andy machine that would sometimes accidentally deposit its sand on the floor. We always got a game or two, Snakes and Ladders being a favourite. The children's books that found their way to our home were not inspiring; *A Child's Garden of Verses* was not enthralling. I liked books that had more real stuff and pictures, something by Ernest Thompson Seton perhaps.

Usually the Christmas loot did not see us very far into winter. The wallpaper sample book did though. Wallpaper books were not large then, maybe about ten inches by fifteen and the paper was sturdy. Oh, those hours we spent on the bedroom floor as we chose which pretty paper would be the side of the building and which paper would be the roof, plain of course. We became quite expert at designing and making free-standing buildings held together with generous lashings of flour and water paste. We built whole villages and barns and henhouses and even a pigpen. Our oldest sister, Jean, was an absolute genius at providing the requisite farm animals. She would take a piece of light-weight cardboard and, without the use of a drawn outline, would quickly cut out any animal desired, perfect specimens of their genre. They would have four separate legs and by spreading them we had animals that stood in various poses. A few years ago, when she visited, I told her of my warm memory of our wallpaper buildings and the animals that she made for our farms. I asked if she could still do it. She took the scissors and the cardboard and, lo and behold, the perfect horse, the perfect cow, the perfect pig. I mailed them to her son not long ago as a wonderful memento of his mother. He had not known of her distinctive skill.

Sometimes we would be scooted off to the real barn up on the hill. It must have been a treat to get us out of the house. I'm sure our mother never knew how we played up there. The high hayloft was filled with hay in the summer (and that is another story). There were oat sheaves too. My father liked to keep his livestock well fed. As the winter progressed, the hay supply would get farther and farther back in the big loft and it was a challenge to climb the vertical face of it and get to the top. First up was king and had the privilege of knocking back all comers. Eventually, though, we would all be up there near the roof. Then the real fun began. The cross-beams at the peak of the roof could be reached. The game was to grip a cross-beam and then the next and the next until we had swung out over the empty part of the hayloft away down below. Not one of us ever fell; there must be a special angel whose domain is haylofts!

One memorable summer Uncle Jim, our mother's bachelor brother, and the provider of everything substantial, bought us a bicycle. Oh, that bicycle. He, or she, who got to ride it was the envied one. It took that special person the two and a quarter miles to school in the summer. It gave us a total new freedom. I recall vividly my own special ride on it. Our father had made a scraper for keeping the weeds off the tennis court that had been wrested from the thick prairie grass near our front yard. I don't recall the reason for the scraper being at our neighbour's, but I was sent one day to bring it back the three miles on the bicycle. It was a heavy, unwieldy thing with a long, sturdy metal-pipe handle, a big blade and metal wheels. I balanced it carefully across the handlebars and started home, up and down the rolling hills. All went well until I came to a steep, newly graded hill about half way home. The only brake on the bicycle was the backward pressure on the pedal. As I started down the long hill the bicycle gathered momentum, fueled by the weight of the scraper. The feeble braking system did not deter the forward momentum; the bicycle began to weave violently from one side of the road to the other. I could not control it as it went faster and faster on its erratic path. How I survived that wild ride, I will never know. I think my salvation was that the trail had been newly graded and widened. There was a considerable drop to each side but my bicycle guardian angel was obviously riding with me that day! It was not my riding skill that kept me alive.

My bicycle guardian angel had to be with me almost every day I rode the bicycle to school. About half way there I had to ride past my aunt's house. Once again, there were two steep hills to navigate. One, the shorter, dipped down to a slough where sometimes a bull would be tethered to graze. But he was not the big hazard; the big hazard was my aunt's pack of hounds. The hounds lazed around all summer; they were used in the winter to catch coyotes. They were an ugly, mongrel lot; I hated every one of them. A bicycle invading their territory was a signal for the chase. Not as good as a coyote, but it would have to do. I soon learned to not pedal; my moving legs were a target. So I coasted down the hill and prayed that I had enough momentum to keep me going down the next longer one. If I rode looking straight ahead, not moving a muscle, the chase became boring for the dogs and I had escaped once again. I complained to my mother about the hounds but nothing came of it. They were my aunt's pets and could do no harm. I am thankful they didn't! To this day I am afraid of big dogs, especially hounds.

On sunny days in the summer we played outside with what nature provided, stones. We did not have a stony farm, but there were plenty of pebbles. We would gather these near the barn; the large ones were the horses and the others different animals according to size. We would lay out our barn and our pasture using straw to indicate the boundaries and the stalls. There were disputes, of course, about the stones: colour, smoothness and size being the major considerations.

There was one larger stone I especially remember, not as a plaything in the pebble-farm mix, but because it was so different. It was about five inches long, a round oblong with smooth tapered ends. It was dull grey, not pretty at all but it had one characteristic that made it unique: a smooth hole about three quarters of an inch in diameter midway right through it so it would be well balanced. The edges of the hole were worn smooth all around. In retrospect, it was probably an ancient weapon and it is probably still there today, waiting for the right finder with the required perception.

While the winter had its wallpaper buildings for inside play and the barn loft its aerobic challenges, the great winter outdoors in Saskatchewan provided thrills galore. Once again, Uncle Jim supplied the vehicle, the longest toboggan I ever saw. It had ropes down the sides to hang onto and six of us could squeeze on. The big, long, steep hill by the barn provided the ideal terrain. The steepest part of the hill faced south-east with the usual slough at the bottom. It was an ideal location for drifts to form and form they did; the almost constant winds swirled and banked the snow hard around the hill. It formed successive drifts hard as stone. Like waves in a storm the sharp crests slanted downward, shelter for jackrabbits.

When we set the big toboggan in motion at the top of the hill we knew we were in for a wild ride. The weight of the toboggan made it gain momentum fast and, in no time at all, it was leaping from one rock-hard drift to another, with the riders riding the drifts with shrieking delight. The long toboggan would lift off through the air and, on one particularly wild ride, with five of us aboard, it turned completely around in midair, finally hitting the frozen slough going backward and spilling its screaming cargo in reckless abandon. Not a bone was broken, miracle of miracles!

I sometimes wonder if our parents were oblivious or just indifferent to the dangers involved in our play. Did they sit there in the living room, my mother knitting, my father reading or listening on the earphones to the Marconi radio, unaware that our childhood pleasures sometimes bordered on the lethal. I wonder.

Haying

Of all the work we as children had to do on the farm, I think haying was the worst. For one thing, it was always hot. My father would take the mowing machine, pulled by a team, to the quarter section just west of us; it was known as the Hudson's Bay Quarter and at that time was not farmed. He would mow the native grass called prairie wool that covered the rolling land; it was the staple winter feed for the cows and horses. He would also mow the coarse slough grass that grew tall and thick after the sloughs dried. Slough grass was not nourishing feed, more like roughage but it was the hay I preferred to put up, as haying was called. It had no spears like the prairie wool; the spears developed when the prairie wool went to seed, and they dug in like porcupine quills; they hurt even through the black wool stockings we had to wear for protection as we tramped the hay in the hayrack. We started tramping hay as young as five years old. There is an old housekeeping maxim: "Keep the corners clean and the rest of the house will take care of itself." That maxim could also be applied to haying: "Tramp the corners down well and you'll get a bigger load." We were the corner trampers and we learned young!

After mowing, my father used a wide, team-pulled rake to form it into piles. He had to work with one eye on the weather. If hay was put up even a trifle damp, spontaneous combustion could set the whole barn ablaze. So we had to do the hated haying while it was hot. I remember riding in the empty hayrack to the field, looking up at the blazing sun in the empty sky and hoping for even one small cloud. It didn't usually happen.

Our big loft had an extension built out from the peak of the roof for the purpose of accommodating the haylift that would carry the hay upward and position it in the loft. But a haylift had never been installed and child power had to suffice. It was a terrible job. Our father would lift the hay by forkfulls into the hayloft door and my sisters and I would relay it back, working hard to keep up. At first, when the loft was empty, we could slide the hay along the wood floor to the far end, but that didn't last long, we had to start lifting it up and up. The bone dry speargrass was dusty; soon we could hardly see each other through the haze. There was no ventilation in the loft except through the small door that our father used. Our arms ached, our throats were parched, as our father exhorted us to keep up. There would be three of us: Lois, Jean and me. The most desirable position was the one near the door which allowed a brief respite of fresh air. I recall thinking I could not possibly lift another forkful as perspiration drenched my cotton dress, and the hated black wool stockings became pale with the spears that were more like attack weapons.

Hayracks were wide, cumbersome things with wide woodslats across the ends and slanted toward the middle on the sides, making them easier to load. They were built of rough wood and that could be a hazard, as I found out when riding an empty one; the road was rutted and I hung on to the two-by-four in the front; the hayrack lurched, my hand slid and the palm of it ended up black with slivers. Mother took a sewing needle from the kitchen curtain, where she always kept them, and told me to hold out my hand. I cried; I knew the pain of a needle removing slivers, and there were so many to remove. I pleaded with my mother, "Please, can't we let them fester and then we can squeeze them out." Sensibly, she did not heed my pleading but it was an ordeal (probably for both of us) that I never forgot.

Bringing in the oat sheaves from the field was almost fun compared with haying. The sheaves would have been stooked some time, at least long enough to allow the field mice to set up housekeeping in them. Our little terrier, Tiny, loved following the hayrack as the oat sheaves were gathered. She would wait beside the stook, panting in anticipation of a mouse nest full of delectable pink young mice. Mmm . . . good! Some of the sheaves would be stored in the loft and the rest stacked outside. The same pertained to hay, once the loft was full, the excess hay would be stacked outside. As with so many other endeavours, building a secure stack of oat sheaves required know-how. We were taught early to place the sheaves in such a manner that a well-built stack resisted wind and moisture, rain or snow.

One bright fall day, I was carefully placing the oat sheaves that my father threw up to me when I heard a far off sound with which I was not familiar; I ignored it at first because my father did not take lightly to frivolous interruptions, but when it became louder, I finally drew it to his attention. He stopped and listened; the source of the sound could not be identified, but we knew it was coming from a north-easterly direction. As we listened, a speck appeared in the sky and, to our amazement, an object materialized and flew through the clear sky toward us . . . an airplane! We stared in fascination as it flew low, right over us, the deafening sound requiring my father to hold tight the reins of the frightened horses. We could plainly see the pilot in the open cockpit and I am sure that our awe and wonder amused him. It was an unforgettable introduction to the new flying machine. We stared as it disappeared to the south-west. We never did know the make or the name of the airplane, or Aeroplane, as it was called then; nor did we have any opportunity to ride in it as it made its appearances at prairie fairs where it took up the brave for a price: one cent a pound.

My father prided himself on keeping his livestock clean and well fed. The prairie wool hay was the basic feed, with oat sheaves second, threshed oats third and the occasional scoop of wheat bran a treat. But my father overdid the winter feeding in the case of a fine new Percheron he had just acquired; Dan had a shiny russet coloured coat and, amongst our plodding Clydes he was smooth and handsome; my father pampered him. Alas, it was Dan's undoing. Too much rich feed and not enough exercise (it was a bitterly cold winter) caused him to founder. The veterinary and Dad made a sling that supported Dan. Dad plied him with his faithful Dr. Bell's medicine but to no avail. Dan died. We never had another horse of Dan's calibre and Rock, Rose, Daisy, Bell, Jerry, Mack, Prince, Mae, Dolly, prosaic all, had to carry on. Dolly had a strong maternal instinct that produced twins. Alas, twin foals often do not survive, and as Dolly had foaled sooner than anticipated, they died soon after birth. But by this time in prairie farm history, the tractor was taking over.

After his first venture with the tractor, when he found it could not navigate the steep hills, my father never gave tractors another try. His sons were certainly not into the care and feeding of horses; nor were they born farmers. Perhaps if they had been the eldest in the family things might have been different, but "Timing is everything" and in this case my parents' timing in the gender of their children was crucial; the four first girls worked inside and out, the two boys did not work the land at all. But our family was not alone in this; a surprising number of farm families in our part of Saskatchewan fell into this category, girls born first. One wonders why.

Cats! Cats! Cats! We had lots of them, but always in the barn, never in the house. My mother did not allow cats in her house but my father said they were essential to keep down the mice in the barn.

One summer the cat thing seemed to have gotten completely out of hand. Perhaps the tom(s) had neglected a tom's duty of disposing of the newborn kittens. Perhaps the mothers had become extra diligent about protecting them from the toms. But there was no doubt about it, we had too many cats, large and small.

Saturday evenings in the summer were when we went to town ... not all of us because there was a limit to the capacity of the Model T. Of course, the more the merrier when it came to pushing the cranky vehicle up a steep hill, and there were many of those on the sixteen mile trails.

One Saturday night of this particular summer, Mr. Miller, a Harris merchant, remarked to my father that the mice were getting out of hand and he needed a cat. He had mentioned it to the right person. The next day, Sunday, we had a mad, wild cat hunt. They certainly weren't easy to catch, more feral than domestic it seemed.

My father began the hunt by closing all the barn doors to make the operation simple: no escape. But simple it was not. The cats fought like tigers when cornered, even the little ones. My father wore his big winter gauntlet leather gloves and when a cat was finally subdued, it was shoved into a large hemp gunny sack that had contained bran or shorts from the grist mill. Two of us were assigned to guard the cat bag as other cats, large and small, were brought to join them, reluctantly, fighting all the way.

We helped my father carry the cat cargo into the back seat of the car. I didn't go into town with them; I was exhausted from the chase, with many cat scratches needing immediate attention. My mother had stayed aloof from the whole fiasco with a told-you-so look in her eyes for my father.

I don't know how many cats there were in the big bag; we were too busy to count, but there were about as many as the big gunny sack would hold.

When my father arrived in Harris, it was Sunday evening. The town was quiet, not many about. Those were the days when almost everyone went to church. My father drove up to the closed Miller store which had an unlocked lean-to at the rear. He and his fellow cat hunters deposited the sack inside the lean-to. With agility they untied the bag, backed out, shut the door and bolted it before even one cat escaped.

One last thing, though: they were beautiful cats. My own beloved Daffy was spared deportation, to sire more litters. Daffy had the typical tabby stripes but his coat was a deep orange colour, burnt orange, they used to call it. Most of the cats had the same burnt orange but with black and white also; big patches of well-defined colour, very distinguished.

Finally, we never did hear the reaction of Mr. Miller, the store owner, when the lean-to door was opened the next morning. But mice should no longer be a problem in his store, or anywhere else in the town of Harris. As can be imagined, from that day on, the cat population on our farm was kept strictly under control.

My father had his own definition of marriage: that it was like tying two cats together by their tails and hanging them over a wire fence; that anomaly did not seem to apply to our parents' marriage. By the time I was old enough to be aware, they seemed to have established a peaceful unanimity.

Weeds

In the pre-chemical days of farming, weeds were almost the number one enemy. A weed is defined as "anything that grows where it is not wanted," and they certainly grew where they were not wanted on our farm.

There is one weed I recall, though, with something akin to affection: we called it pigweed, it is listed in my big Webster's dictionary as being "any of certain amaranths." My genteel grandparents called it lamb's quarters which, again in my big dictionary is simply described as pigweed. It seemed to grow everywhere, even down by the pig pen!

The reason for my nostalgic memory of pigweed is that it tasted so good. It was our first feed of greens after a winter of deprivation in that area. Pig weed had to be picked before it seeded and turned bitter. We gathered the young pigweed wherever it could be found and, after it was boiled with a shake of salt, placed on our plates with a generous lashing of butter; it was a culinary delight.

I am surprised that our contemporary fare includes spinach when pigweed (or lamb's quarters) is so much superior. Now, in Toronto, when I go for my daily morning walk and I see young pigweeds by a fence, I have a desire to pick them for a spring treat, but that is not practical; it takes a child's armful of pigweed for a satisfying meal. That, I remember!

Sow thistle (Webster's: "A weed having thistle-like leaves, yellow flowers and milky juice") had no redeeming features. In practical terms, it was a weed to be dreaded, to the extent that government inspectors visited farms that were rumoured to harbour it. My father would take large gunny sacks down to the field and fill them with the hated weed. What he did with it after, I am not sure, but he probably burned it. No farmer liked to admit that he was battling sow thistle; once established, it was almost impossible to eradicate.

Fireweed grew upright near the edge of sloughs, preferring damp ground. As it ripened in the fall, it turned a beautiful russet color, heavy with seed. Woe betide anyone who was subject to hay fever; fireweed was a killer. I recall one fall when my poor aunt could hardly see or breathe. She was awash in the negative effects of fireweed which wouldn't dissipate until the first frost. It was as unpleasant to live with as it was lovely to look at.

Tumbling mustard (Webster's: "Tumbleweed, the branching upper part becomes detached from the roots in autumn and is driven about by the wind.") Well, it was certainly tumbled about by the relentless prairie wind. It grew tall and wide on our farm and, once detached from its root in the fall, it spread its seeds with reckless abandon until it finally settled down for the winter in a convenient fence corner; its fellow travellers tumbled in with it.

My father would have an afternoon's chore on a warm fall day burning the tumbleweed. But when the seven year drought hit the prairies, the tumbling mustard (as it was known), still rolled relentlessly across the barren fields and settled in the same fence corners where it caught the drifting soil that piled higher and higher until the fence posts were buried, sometimes several posts deep. The fellow accomplice in this act of destruction was the hated Russian thistle. (Webster's: "A tumbleweed, growing two to three feet in diameter and having small-leafed spiny branches.")

During the years of drought when feed for the livestock was almost unobtainable, green Russian thistle was harvested for feed, though it was not high in nutrients. At least it kept the animals alive. It, too, broke off when it was ripened and ended up in fence corners adding its bulk to the tumbling mustard. It was no good for feed after it ripened as the spiny branches made it almost impossible for the animals to eat. Like so many plants when their reproduction is threatened, they were prolific with seed. No matter how bleak the growing season, there always seemed to be Russian thistle.

Wild oats (Webster's: "Resembles cultivated oat"), which it did indeed, but the difference to the trained eye was easily discerned: the seed of the wild oat was larger than that of the domesticated and the kernel was thin and poor, having very little feed value. The wild oat plant grew coarse and tall and was thirsty for moisture. It was bad news to have wild oats in a cultivated oat field as, in the case of most weeds, they tried to take over. When the seed was threshed, an infestation of wild oats lowered the crop value.

Foxtail and quack grass seemed to prefer the soil near sloughs. They provided no feed value, were difficult to eradicate and sapped badly needed moisture.

The wild rose had been plentiful on the original prairie where its spreading, sturdy roots nourished it rain or shine. After the prairie sod had been broken, the wild rose was fairly easily eradicated, so it sought refuge by the clumps of buffalo willows that endured in uncultivated areas. We would search for wild rose bushes in the fall so we could feast on the thick red flesh of the seed pods; it was not only good but, as was determined years later, also good for us! In the summer we would gather the pink rose blossoms for our mother who would put them in bowls with a sprinkling of cinnamon for an exquisite pot pourri.

Stinkweed (Webster's: "Any of various rank-smelling plants, also a tree, 'tree of heaven'"). Our particular stinkweed was simply weed that grew about two and a half feet tall with green leaves and bright yellow flowers. The cattle liked stinkweed but it certainly wreaked havoc with their milk. We knew immediately if a cow had found a patch: the milk was undrinkable; for days it tasted dreadful.

I hated pulling stinkweed. In no time we were seemingly oozing the horrible smell from our pores; it was nauseating to handle. We would be sent to the wheat fields in July and ordered to pull every plant from the large patches of stinkweed; there were many. Pulling stinkweed was a punishing way to spend a nice summer day.

I recall one episode where we were sent to pull a stinkweed infestation down near the road. It was a beautiful day and as we toiled pulling the wretched stuff, the neighbour's open Model T car came down the road, the Tyson family on their way to a community picnic. I remember staring at them with envy and dejection as we watched the happy carload off for a day of fun, as they waved cheerily at us. Bitterness filled my child's soul as I turned to my despised duty. Our father never took us on picnics; how I wished that I could be a Tyson!

My favourite little weed is, as far as I am concerned, nameless. It grew in our front yard, a ground cover with an indestructible root system that endured trampling and drought. The animals sometimes nibbled it. This nameless weed was low lying, always green, and had little round leaves. I don't recall that it ever flowered. When all other vegetation failed, this persistent little weed endured. It softened the effect of the hard soil under our bare feet and it provided an always cheery presence. I am sorry I cannot call it by name.

Wheat

When I was a child on the prairies, wheat was king. Our quality of life depended on the success of the wheat crop. There were two varieties that seemed to be favoured; the most popular was Marquis, which is what my father always planted. The other variety was Red Fife which was supposed to have the attribute of being more resistant to rust. Wheat was a sturdy plant but it had many things that plagued it, and at one time or another we seemed to meet them all.

Seed wheat was stored in a special section of our large tri-section granary. About Easter, a fanning mill would be brought in to remove the chaff from the seed. The fanning portion of the mill was turned by hand; it was arduous work, dusty and slow. One spring my sister, Jean, and I were kept home from school for a few days to help with the fanning. We would much rather have been in school!

The reason that particular year remains in my memory is because we received recognition for our labour. Our father went into town shortly after and when he returned he had an Easter egg for each of us. My egg was a big one of brown chocolate with colored flowers on top. It was much too pretty to eat so for a few days it sat on a special shelf in our living room. Finally, I could resist no longer so I broke off a piece of the brown chocolate, just to taste it! My disillusionment was almost unbearable: the egg was hollow. I had pictured a feast of chocolate that would last and last; I had not realized it did not weigh enough to be solid. My memory of the disappointing egg is solidly linked to fanning wheat. I had been paid in spurious coin!

Wheat was always pickled the night before seeding. In the spring evening my father would fill a big wooden barrel with water into which he would empty a jug of liquid formaldehyde. He would stand over the barrel and lower a kegful of wheat into the water. The wooden keg had many drain holes drilled into it so the water drained out rapidly as my father rested the keg over the barrel. He would then empty the keg of pickled grain into the large grain wagon. There was a twofold purpose to pickling grain: the moisture encouraged early germination and the formaldehyde supposedly guarded the grain against fungi such as rust.

Every year there seemed to be something: one year rust kept the wheat kernels from maturing as they should; another, the sawfly entered the stem of the wheat and cut it down, as the name implies, just before ripening. If the crop had grown thick and lush it would topple from its own weight; a lodged crop was almost impossible to harvest in the days of the binder.

Then there was hail. Hail seemed to hit in streaks; there were districts that were known as hail country where a fine crop could be wiped out in minutes. Insurance could be bought to soften the blow in hail country, but the almost prohibitive cost of the insurance discouraged the investment in it. After a severe thunderstorm had gone through, there would be much telephoning among neighbours to spread the good or bad news of the devastation. If a good yield had been expected, the loss was catastrophic.

Then, at the end, there would be frost; a frost when the kernel was in the milk stage meant a lower grade than the coveted A grade. Sometimes a frosted crop would grade 'feed' and the quality of the farm family's living would have to wait until next year for an upgrade.

The rich, loam soil worked by prairie pioneers required two elements: heat and moisture, but those two variables were at the mercy of capricious nature. The first prairie farmers, without benefit of technology or chemicals, lived on hope and faith that the right moisture and the right heat would be provided. Sometimes they were, but more often they were not.

When my father was about to turn the first furrow on new acreage, he would pace it off carefully at each end. Then he would show me where I was to stand as I held high a long pole with a bright cloth on the top. It was his marker to head towards. I stood and stood. The land was what was known as rolling, with dips, hills and valleys. I would have little or no idea how fast the plow was advancing. It seemed to take forever. My father liked things done right so it would be intolerable to have a breaking furrow that was not straight. It was tolerable, though, to make children do work and have responsibilities that were far beyond their strength and their years.

The wheat crop, good or bad, provided us with one of the main essentials of our livelihood: flour. There was a grist mill in Harris that processed the wheat farmers took to it. The big load of sacked flour that my father brought home from the mill in the fall marked the beginning of winter-style living. We kept the hundred-pound bags of flour in the attic over the kitchen. It was the children's job to take the bags as they were lifted up and drag them back, being careful that no slivers from the storage planks caught and made holes in the bags as we dragged them along.

There were residual products from the wheat as well: big bags of bran that weighed much less than the flour. There was also a smaller, heavy bag of what was known as shorts, which I suppose today would be called wheat germ. Most of the shorts and bran were fed to the pigs, but my mother reserved some to vary the white loaves she baked every other day. The last bit of dough would receive a handful or two of bran to make brown bread.

There was never any thought nor discussion about the quality of the food that we ate, no reference to whether it was good for us, or not. No one read the list of ingredients on a can or a bucket. It was taken for granted that the words peanut butter meant that was what it was, simply peanuts. (Now I know how we could have told it was pure, without benefit of ingredient listing: real peanut butter had a generous layer of peanut oil on the top of the ground peanuts. This would have to be mixed to make it spreadable, a chore for a child.) Peanut butter was a staple of every child's school sandwiches and our family went through many pails of it in a year.

Finally, for the children, there was one favourite use of wheat: chewing gum. It took a lot of chewing to reduce a mouthful of wheat to a chewable mass but, from a parent's point of view, there were two positive things about wheat chewing gum. It contained no sugar to endanger our teeth, and it was cheap!

Harvesting

For anyone who works the land for a living, the culmination of their effort is the harvest. After the harvest there is only 'next year' ahead. Saskatchewan has always been known as next year country. The tribulations and plagues that beset the farmers there are legion; from the weather to pests to disease, the crops were vulnerable all down the line. This meant that the farmers' quality of living was always tenuous. The irony was, that on the occasional year when the yield was bountiful, the price would be low; a classic case of supply and demand.

In the horsepower days (when horsepower meant the number of horses, not the power of the engine), farming was a never-ending operation from early spring seeding to the final wagonload of grain in the granary. After the seeding was over, the tilling of the land took up most of the summer. Plowing, even with a large gang-plow, was tedious. Fortunately, our land was not stony, as were many of the neighbouring farms. With stones, your work was never done. Each spring saw a new crop of boulders heaved to the surface by the winter frost. The amount of stone on any quarter was evident by the size of the stone fences that outlined the unfortunate fields. Gathering stones was something that was always waiting to be done. They were hauled by horses on a stoneboat, a piece of equipment that could be found on every farm. A stoneboat was made of sturdy planks on equally sturdy runners and it was the means of transporting everything from barn manure to water barrels to new calves, or even a new harvest of stones!

There was a certain rhythm to the working of the land. Some would be seeded in the spring to provide that year's harvest. A percentage would remain fallow so it could be prepared during the summer for the next spring's seeding. After the stubble from the previous year's crop had been plowed, it would be disced to break up the furrows and then harrowed; sometimes a second harrowing would be required for weed control.

If the weather permitted after the harvest, my father would do some fall plowing. In the fall of 1931, after my mother had left early in October to have her baby in Rosetown, the weather remained fine so my father was able to plow. Iris, the baby, was tardy in arriving, and my father remarked that our mother would be pleased with what he had done. How sad that she never saw it. But at least she was spared the agony of seven years of drought and depression that lay ahead.

The tedium of riding slow, horse-drawn machinery on a hard, metal seat was wearying in the extreme, even though the seat was cushioned by well-anchored, well-worn sheepskin. No wonder my father came in from the field dog tired. In the hiatus between the harrow and the binder, there was ample work to fill a farmer's day: there was always fence-mending, building maintenance and haying.

As with everything that is dependent on the weather, the time of harvest varied, but the first swath of the binder was usually made on a hot day. I remember it well. My sisters and I were the stookers. The binder would spit out heavy sheaves of wheat or oats, bound with binder twine. There was a knack to stooking: it was heavy work. We used a three-tined fork to lift the sheaves, anchor the first two on their straw ends against each other, then two opposite, and on that foundation we built the sheaves around so the stook stood securely against wind and rain. A well stooked field is a lovely sight and only a person who has stooked knows the physical cost. I was always sick the first day of stooking; working hard in the hot sun, my body rebelled and I would crouch behind a stook and bring up everything I had eaten. After the first day of being sick, I adjusted to the hard labour in the hot sun, but invariably I would be sick the first day. That's what I remember most about stooking!

Naturally, we could not keep up to the binder, so hired help would be brought in. Usually they were men who had gone west from eastern Canada for the harvest, but native Indians would sometimes appear at the farm, looking for harvest work. The quality of the harvest help varied greatly. One year we had an agricultural student from the university who viewed the harvest work as part of the curriculum. He knew what he was doing and was a dedicated worker . . . a real find. Men who had been employed elsewhere as loggers, or who had never harnessed a horse, were a challenge. I recall one couple, a man and a woman, who came to help my father and mother. They were given the bedroom that my older sister and I shared. The couple were indifferent workers and there was no regret on either side when their stint at harvesting was over. My sister and I reclaimed our room. Imagine our chagrin when we searched through our dresser drawers for favourite pieces of clothing and found them gone. The item that I lamented the most was a burnt orange coloured pullover sweater that had been knit by my mother. It was one of my prized possessions . . . gone. Whenever I think of farm hired help, I remember my beautiful sweater. It was mean of that woman to take it; my mother had been kind and patient with her. It was a hard-earned lesson for me: being good to people does not ensure that they will be good to you! It was my first brush with theft.

Following the reaping and the stooking, we waited for the threshers to come. The threshing outfits made their slow way from farm to farm. Usually the outfits were family owned and, naturally, they did their own fields first. My father would have made his reservation well ahead, but the actual threshing date was contingent on the weather (isn't everything in farming?). Depending on the capability of the crew, the reliability of the machinery, and barring accidents, it was possible to predict when, and how long, the threshing crew would be at our farm.

The day started early during threshing, about 4:30 a.m., when my mother would rise to start the kitchen stove to prepare an early breakfast for the hungry crew. There would be eight or ten men in all, including the field hands who gathered the sheaves in horse-drawn hayracks. A full load would be taken to the separator, which ate them up and spat out the straw and the grain. Huge strawstacks would be blown out and piled high at a safe distance from the fire hazard created by the hot, moving, metal of the big machines. Horses new to threshing, were scared of the moving belt and the noise of the whole operation. It was no place for a spooky horse, nor for a green workman. Put together a town boy and a pair of skittish broncos and you had a recipe for disaster; it happened, but not too often.

Everyone kept their fingers crossed that it didn't rain (wet sheaves could not be threshed), or that nothing broke down; repairs were many miles away, or even unobtainable. The engineer was the key man, and he knew it!

One fall the threshing outfit at our farm were nearing the end, one more day would do it. But that day would be a Sunday, so my father decreed that they would not work on that day, but would finish on the Monday. The timing was bad, it started to rain, and it rained and it rained. My poor mother had to feed that threshing crew for thirteen straight days before the last bit of threshing could be finished. It was a costly harvest. It must have been a long, boring spell for the crew, confined to their bunkhouse. But I know that they were pleased to be marooned at the Giffords', if marooned they must be: my mother fed them well in contrast to some of the places they worked.

There is a story that at one penurious farm family, when the threshers came in for lunch, they found a bowl of hard boiled eggs in the centre of the table, one egg to each man!

In the early days of lush crops, farmers prided themselves on high, dense growth, rather than on the yield and quality of the heads of grain. Too bad that the heavy straw was not utilized as mulch but, instead, was often burned.

After the threshers had gone, we had the big, golden straw stacks to explore. On one occasion, the last wagon load of wheat had been left down by the straw stack. It was almost dark when my father told me to take the team and go and bring the wagon in. It was a little distance from the buildings and I did not realize until I approached it over a hill that my father had already set fire to the fresh straw stack. The wagon stood close by; the horses almost balked at going that close to the fire. I finally managed to get them hitched to the wagon of grain. I have thought after that it was a dreadful thing to do to a child (I would have been about 12), exposing me to the double danger of bolting horses and burning straw swirling through the air. It would never have occurred to me to go back and say I could not do it. My father's word was law.

It was interesting that many farmers decided they would burn on the same night. Our prairie horizon would be adorned with bright jewels of flame ascending from the straw stacks; an unforgettable sight, but a short-lived one: combines eliminated straw stacks. They also eliminated great play places: to crawl to the very top and roll down was fall frolic. It was sad when their turn came to be burned.

It was a school day in the fall when our teacher, Mr. Lyon, announced that the whole school would go down the road to watch something we had not seen before. He was right, we had not: it was a combine, making its first rounds of a field of wheat. Too bad we did not have a camera with us; it would be a short-lived sight, a horse-drawn combine. It was the precursor of the famed self-propelled combine where the operator controlled it from on high, like the captain of a ship. The day of the horse came to an abrupt halt.

A swather would cut the grain and lay it in windrows; the combine would gather it and thresh as it moved slowly along, spewing the straw out behind. The combine was a wonderful innovation, but it changed the face of the prairies forever. As one year ran into another, technology improved the combine until today a friend my age tells me that he, his son-in-law, and a nephew can, by themselves, harvest a crop on land so extensive it was once the home of eight farm families. Eight farm families gone!

Today, when I drive the once familiar terrain, I am a stranger; the land has reverted. The old farm buildings that bordered the roads are derelict or gone, miles and miles are bare of any habitation. It is as though the prairie has gone back to its original emptiness. Present day farms have become so large, the machinery so massive, efficient, (and costly!) that, like modern factories, human hands are no longer required.

On my last visit, the bleakness of the landscape was accentuated when I saw, near my Uncle John's abandoned homestead, at a distance across a stubble field, an antelope. I had never before seen an antelope in our part of the prairies: antelopes lived on the southern plains of Alberta. But there it was, making a statement. There was so little evidence of human settlement, the wild animals were taking over and advancing into new territory. That is what the prairies seem to have become, unoccupied, wild. Fences have come down, no need for them, no livestock. The land is tilled with mighty machines, to the last inch of permissiveness, along road allowances. Every effort is directed toward the ultimate in utility.

My grandfather's buildings still stand, wind-swept of all paint; the barn is sway-backed, the house, originally sod then sheathed with wood siding, is uninhabitable, except for the ghosts that knew it when it embraced love and laughter; mean winds blow through open doors and windows. The old buildings huddle there, waiting for a kind lightning bolt to strike and obliterate them in a blaze of glory: the ultimate harvest.

But back to my father's everyday reality of raising a crop: the fanning, pickling, seeding, late spring sleet, cold weather that slowed germination, summer's heat, drought, weeds (the dreaded sow thistle, stinkweed, fireweed, Russian thistle), cutworm, wireworm, sawfly, gophers, rust, lodging grain, breakdowns, sick animals, poor harvest weather; when all that had been endured and overcome, it was time to take the harvest to market.

It did seem cruel that after working so hard all summer, taking the grain to market was a long, miserable haul in the winter. My father would rise long before daylight, hitch the team to the sleigh he had loaded with about sixty bushels of wheat the day before, then set out on the mean winter trail. But at least he would not be alone for long, others would join the trek to the grain elevators in Harris. Once arrived, they sometimes faced a long cold wait in the line outside the elevator. Finally the horses got their reward in the town's livery stable where the drivers would congregate to curse the Winnipeg Grain Exchange, which no doubt had shafted them once again on the price.

To face the bitter prairie wind, the grain-haulers wore full-length buffalo skin coats. Their hats were muskrat skins, lined with earflaps tied under the chin. Their metal-buckled overshoes were quite inadequate against the awful cold. To prevent his feet from freezing, my father would walk many of the sixteen miles beside the sleigh. His hands were protected by leather gauntlet mitts reinforced with my mother's hand-knitted liners. The only time he would remove the mitts was to light a comforting hand-rolled cigarette.

After the sojourn at the livery stable, his next stop would be at Marshall's General Store where he filled our mother's list of necessities: big cardboard boxes of dried fruits, prunes, dates, apricots, raisins, currants, even figs. The sugar came in hundred-pound fine cotton bags, and sago and tapioca for puddings were a family favourite. General Store meant just what it said. The stock was eclectic, basic to the needs of a community that depended on it for almost every need from coal oil for the lamps to perhaps a box of chocolates for the 'little woman' if the price of the grain had been right! There were two general stores in Harris; The Millar store and the Marshall store. The Millar store catered somewhat to a female clientele; fancy writing paper and dressmaking patterns with instructions called deltors. Naturally, my father dealt mostly at Bill Marshall's.

The biggest competitor the two stores had was the Eaton catalogue. Farmers were not above throwing up Eaton catalogue prices to the local merchant. A story is told about a certain farmer who wanted to buy a new axe. When the merchant named his price for the one in stock, the buyer complained that he could get it at a much lower price from the catalogue. The merchant told him he could have it at that price, then he laid it away behind the counter. The farmer asked what he was doing, the merchant answered "Come back and get it the same day you would have received it from the catalogue."

All of our fuel had to be hauled from town. The quality of the coal was important, Drumheller anthracite being the favourite. Anthracite burned with a minimum of ashes and cinders, was long lasting and hot. Firewood had to be bought (no trees on the prairie) and it was the children's duty in summer to split the kindling; a nasty chore if the wood had many knots. We all tried to get out of it but then when I think of it, for children of the pioneers, farm life seemed to be one long nasty chore!

Sloughs

My Webster's dictionary defines the word slough in this manner: "An area of soft, muddy ground." Sloughs were an integral part of the Canadian prairie. To try to define them in a narrow context, would seem to be almost impossible. Each slough had its own personality.

There were several on our farm but when we referred to The Slough, we were referring to the big one that lay just south-west of our house. I could calculate that it covered an acre. Actually, it was located on my Aunt Hat's land. For some reason, our father had built his house just a few feet inside his property line. This meant, for instance, that the ashpile for our stove and heater ashes was partially on Aunt Hat's land as well. I think they had made some sort of arrangement whereby we had the use of her land that contained the big slough because, in that area, we also had our vegetable garden, the tennis court, and even our clothes line paralleled the property line.

Melted winter snows filled the slough, and a good heavy rain could restore it in the summer, even after its stagnant waters had receded. It was a fascinating place for a child, especially in the spring. I recall standing, by myself, on the very edge of a hard, sharply curved snow bank that hung right over the newly melted water, and peering down. If the snow had given away, I would have tumbled into the ice-cold depths, and that would have been the end of me. I wonder if my mother knew of the danger of letting a lone child explore the treacherous spring slough.

After the slough had filled completely in the spring, and the weather was mild, it was a delight to get into the rowboat that my father had built and navigate the length and breadth of the large body of water. Neighbours, who had come for their mail, would often join us; none could swim, but there was never an accident, and I realize now that the kind Slough Gods were with us. But rowing on the slough was a short-term pleasure. As sloughs are not spring-fed, and are entirely stagnant water, evaporation soon took its toll. Willows lined the edges and grasses soon encroached on the shores. Stagnant water means mosquitoes; millions and millions of mosquitoes. In order to combat them, municipalities used oil slicks on the water surface to try to control reproduction, but the effort was only partially successful. Having a slough nearby meant mosquitoes!

In the heat of the summer, the slough would be further depleted when my father hauled barrels of it on the stoneboat to pour on the garden. By the time he got around to doing this, the garden soil was usually bone dry so most of the water would simply run off. What remained caused a hard crust to form and that choked the vegetables almost to extinction. It seemed an exercise in futility, but he repeated it almost every summer.

The lower the level of water in the slough, the muddier it became, until we were finally swimming in a brown sludge that was reduced to the width of the channel formed by the stoneboat that had taken water to the garden. But we still loved its wetness.

The slough usually expired just when it was needed the most. Rainfall would then have to fill the needs of our family for washing clothes, hair and bodies. Rainfall on the prairies was unreliable. In dire need, my mother would dump a can of lye into the big metal barrel of hard well water and, after the lye had settled, the water could be used for washing clothes. If the rain barrels at the corners of the house remained dry, my father would hitch a team to the wagon, load on the dry rain barrels and take the long trail to fill the barrels from a reliable slough up in The Hills. By this time, the summer heat had dried the wooden barrels, and I remember the precious, soft water that leaked from them on the trip home.

In the winter, after the fall rains (that played such havoc with harvesting), some sloughs again held water. There was one unique slough north of us that covered quite an area. In the coldest part of winter, we would go there with the horses and sleigh and my father and neighbours would cut huge blocks of ice. I liked that slough; it was unique because it had muskrats in it. Their well-built houses, made of reeds, twigs and mud, extended above the ice surface. Though I never saw a muskrat, we knew they were there. The local young men trapped them for their hides; muskrat skins made popular fur coats for women. When my mother was young, she and her sisters and her mother each had a muskrat coat, purchased no doubt after a good crop year.

As children, my sisters and I had intimate knowledge of every slough on our property. Some sloughs were surrounded by tall poplar trees that crows favoured for nests. Willows bordered almost every slough. In the heat of the summer, we would take lunches in tin pails down to a slough where we would hunt for wild strawberries and wade if there was wading water. But some sloughs were just barren depressions after the water was gone; they yielded heavy crops of slough grass, but it was not nutritious feed for the animals. Some slough grass would be put in the loft for winter: it looked good, but apparently not to the ruminants; cows would not eat it.

Shallow sloughs that dried early could be tilled and the growth in them would be rank, so rank, in fact that it often would lodge, making it impossible to harvest. The rolling hills on our land meant that we had lots of sloughs; our grandfather's land was largely flat so sloughs were not a problem (or a blessing!) to them.

I liked sloughs, they provided diversity and they were great to play around and in. For us, when we were children, they were certainly not Bunyan's famed, "Slough of Despair."

After the dry years on the prairies, farmers provided themselves with substitute sloughs: dugouts. These were deep excavations, usually on the farm yards, and they were storage areas for scarce soft water from the winter snows and the rain.

Dugouts were surprisingly effective as they held the water well without lining. Little growth invaded the steep sides and, if it did, was easily controlled. Of course, nothing is ever without a negative. In the case of the dugouts, children could drown in them, and some did. But then, children also drowned in sloughs: high on a hilltop in southern Saskatchewan, a wooden cross marks the graves of two young pioneer boys who drowned in the slough at the foot of the hill. Graveyards and churches were still in the future on the prairies so their grieving parents buried them, without ceremony, near where they had died.

The only fresh, moving water to which we had access, was a creek, Eagle Creek, about eight miles south-west of our farm. In the spring, the runoff coming down from the far Rockies, combined with melting snow to turn the creek into a torrent. The creek bed was deep, and at one time in its history, the creek had cut a wide swath of about a quarter of a mile through the prairie. A bridge spanned Eagle Creek, but was useless when the creek was in full flood. In the heat of summer, it had a popular swimming hole with big boulders to climb on and water of varying depth.

When I think of Eagle Creek, however, I think of my grandfather Elder studying a map in the Land Settlement Office in Saskatoon, the spring of 1905. A clerk showed him the map of the area that was open for homesteading. A squiggly line crossed through the map and my grandfather asked what it meant. The clerk replied, "Oh, that's just an Indian trail." Imagine my grandfather's surprise when he found later, as he searched on foot for a homestead, that the Indian trail was in fact a deep, wide, rushing body of water, length unknown! There was another landmark body of water not far from us, it was called Bitter Lake, with good reason. It was a lake of good size, if not of good water, the taste so unpalatable, no one ever ventured into the water. But it looked pretty.

One year a community picnic was held beside it. To get to the picnic site, rutted roads had to suffice. We went in the buggy which at times tilted perilously on the side of the hills: I was afraid. No settlement was near the lake, discouraged, no doubt by the putrid smell of the waters. But the picnic was a success, nonetheless: baseball was played; the contents of the picnic baskets enjoyed; treats were bought at the small concession booth, and the gossip that flowed made the day at Bitter Lake sweet indeed.

We suffered from a lack of ice for skating in the winter. Ordinary sloughs did not hold their water long enough to form ice, and those that did would be so shallow the long slough grass protruded. I do not know if Bitter Lake provided ice for skating: it was too distant. Occasionally, we went to Harris to skate in their arena, where we were immediately identified as inept country invaders, and thus open to derision.

Sky

The 'Big, Blue Sky' cliche about the prairies holds little charm for me. Big and Blue usually meant hot. Riding on the hayrack, going out to the east quarter for hay, I would scan the sky, hopeful that even a tiny cloud would shield us for even a few minutes from the merciless sun. We took for granted the fact that the air was clear and unadulterated, except those, of course, who suffered from pollen allergies. Now that I have lived in a thoroughly polluted area for many years, I appreciate, in hindsight, the purity of the prairie air.

Pollution is blamed for many human ailments, such as cancer and asthma. Then, I ask myself, why did my Aunt Bessie, at age 30, contract cancer in the pristine pure prairie: no air pollution, no chemical pollution, no stress, none of the villains that are accused of causing so much cancer now in later years. In 1923, cancer was not spoken about in polite society. It was not respectable to do so, especially as, in the case of my aunt, it was cancer of the breast. She was sent to the Mayo Clinic in Rochester, Minnesota, for treatment. They operated, sent her home to Saskatchewan, and said that she would live for about a year, which was accurate. There is an interesting follow-up to her stay at the Mayo Clinic. When my grandfather was sent the final bill, and he protested that it was excessive, he was told that they had investigated his financial status and that they only charged him in ratio to what they thought he could pay.

My grandmother suffered from that other disease, asthma, that is today supposedly pollution oriented; it eventually caused her death. On the prairie, rust does not destroy every piece of metal it can invade. On a shelf in an outdoor shed on my grandfather's farm, along with tins of nails and other metal sundries, I found a tin not many years ago that had contained my grandmother's asthma medication, a powder. It was empty, but the orange coloured, tall, slim tin was in perfect condition. The instructions for the use of the medicine were printed on the side, together with an early 20th century picture of an asthma sufferer, female. The instructions read, in part, that it was to be smoked in a clean, clay pipe! My dear niece, Joan, in Vancouver, is involved in the field of medicine. I packaged the tin and sent it to her; she loved it, but regretted that a clean, clay pipe was not included.

One advantage of the prairies: we did not suffer the sullen skies that obliterate the sun so many days of the year where homes are adjacent to water. But there were many, many days when I would have gladly traded the cheery sun for the mist of the water. It is often noted that the prairies produce writers. My theory is that the unlimited sky and the seemingly limitless horizon influence thought projection; imaginations are extended. I think of the elderly woman who moved to the Rockies after long years on the prairies. Someone asked her if she liked living in the mountains. I understand her reply, "Oh, if they would just kneel down sometimes so I could see over."

There was one memorable day when I saw much farther than I could comprehend. It was a summer morning and I was walking to school. (Our summer holiday was July, our winter holiday, January, no spring break.) On this particular morning I had not walked far when suddenly the whole south-west skyline was alive with people: people going out to the barn, people pumping water, people herding animals, people doing all the morning things that are done on a farm. Towns and their tall elevators were everywhere. I stood and experienced the diorama in wonder and disbelief. I felt that I could call out to the people and would be heard. I do not remember how long it lasted. I never saw a mirage of that scope again, and I was certainly privileged to witness that one. Now, when I hear tales of the mirages of the desert, I do not dispute them; I had a fact-defying mirage of my own.

Everyone raised in the crystal clear air of the prairies in the early part of the century, can tell tales of the aurora borealis. We did not call it that; to us it was simply the northern lights. The northern lights were common, but not so common that we took them for granted. When someone came in on a cold winter's night and said, "Come out and see the northern lights," we went. What a spectacle they could be as they literally danced across our northern sky, so full of motion and so extensive, it was difficult to assimilate it in one sighting. They seemed alive. Although known to sometimes make a crackling sound, the northern lights we saw were always silent. I think it would have added fear to our awe if there had been sound. It is difficult to imagine any other natural sight with the mesmerizing grandeur of the northern lights on the prairies on an especially good night.

Our family had acquired a radio, a big, wide Marconi that had a horn on top and operated on the strength of large cylindrical batteries. There were earphones that my mother wore as she listened to the radio after we had all gone to bed.

My mother kept a log of the radio stations she heard and I wish I had it today, but it was discarded with no thought of its historical content. I know that KOA Denver was one of her regular favourites and that she had logged stations as far south as Brazil. I recall that there was a connection between the radio reception and the northern lights; the northern lights caused static. Personally, I was not an enthusiast of the radio: music would blare from the big, black horn when I was trying to do homework, offending my tin ear.

Not everything about the sky was ethereal or benign. There were storms that swept across the open plain like banshees from hell. When a storm threatened, that threat was taken seriously, especially if it bore a hint of hail. We had no advance warnings via radio or television. After the advent of the radio, my mother always said she could tell what our weather would be: it would be Edmonton's, 24 hours later.

One summer night we were awakened in our bedroom by our parents; a storm raged outside and they were afraid that our wooden home could not withstand its velocity. Their obvious state of alarm scared us. We cowered under the covers as our father put a large sheet of something, like a canvas, over us to provide some protection. Fortunately, the roof held, but it was a close call. Fierce winds could suddenly sweep across the wide prairie with nothing to impede nor divert them; they were treated with fear and respect. A cyclone did take our barn, well, part of our barn. It was in the process of construction, the side walls and the rafters were up when a summer cyclone hit in the night. I have pictures of the destruction.

My father was a careful builder, but after the cyclone he took no second chance. When the barn was rebuilt, he used ploughshares, buried in the cement of the barn floor, and attached them with heavy wires to the roof rafters. Even though it sat exposed on a high hill, no storm laid waste to it thereafter. Once the barn was completed, neighbours came from far and near to the traditional barn-opening party. I was young, but just old enough to have vague recollections of it.

Once, when I was an adult, my father and I had a conversation about our farm house. I mentioned that I remembered the big hole for the cellar under the new kitchen. I told him about standing on its edge and being afraid. He told me I could not possibly remember that: I was only a year and a half old at the time. But it was an authentic memory, not something someone had told; there would be no cause to mention a minor event like the digging of a cellar. He had to believe me.

Our kitchen windows faced west so we felt the full impact of the famed prairie sunsets. One well known artist has rated the prairie sunsets on a par with those of Mexico. Like most things in life, with which we are familiar, we took them for granted. Often they were spectacular, but there was one special summer sunset I will never forget. It was just before dark and the sun had gone down. My mother told me to bring in the turkey hen and her brood. They had settled down for the night in the stubble and if she had been allowed to stay, she and the little ones would have been a breakfast for the coyotes. We knew that, but the turkey did not; she was reluctant to be brought into the safety of the secure hen-house. I found her without much difficulty, but then a strange thing happened: the whole world turned purple. In the last reflecting rays of the sun, an atmospheric phenomenon had caused the sky to turn purple, not just the sunset part of the sky,

but the whole sky from the north horizon to the south and from
the west to the east. It was like walking through colour with a mist-
iness to it that added to the unreality. It was not mauve, but true
purple, even the turkey hen was cowed by it. It lasted for perhaps
fifteen minutes and then abated.

The closest I came to experiencing the intensity of that colour
experience again was in Toronto. I was working downtown, had
gone from University Avenue to Yonge Street and was returning to
do some extra work in the evening. It was a misty time of day, not
unusual so close to Lake Ontario. The new City Hall buildings had
been completed not long before and there was an unimpeded view
of the two crescent-shaped buildings as I walked west on a street
two blocks directly south. As I came opposite, I stopped and stared.
A mist had enveloped and obscured the bottom part of the large,
grey buildings. As I looked at them across the open space of the
big, public square, it seemed that the buildings had been cast from
their moorings and were floating in a sea of mauve mist. I could
scarcely believe what I was seeing, it was so ethereally beautiful, and
I knew I would never see it again. (My unimpaired view would soon
be filled with buildings). I stood alone on the sidewalk staring; I
felt blessed.

Dances

The rural schoolhouse was the social centre of the community.
During the winter, every Friday night a 'do,' as they were called,
would be held in one schoolhouse or another. The young people
travelled many miles to attend: some districts held dos that were
much livelier than others. The two schoolhouses in our sphere,
Ailsa Craig and Hillview, were usually attended by an older crowd
who were inclined to be subdued and proper. Cards (whist) were
played very seriously, the winners advancing to another table so
there was a circulation of players and the gossip did not get stale.
Prizes would be awarded to the winners, who were usually predictable. After the card games, entertainment in the form of recita-
tions and musical offerings would be given. Once again, they were

somewhat predictable as, after all, there was not a large pool of talent from which to draw. Uncle Jim often gave a reading or a recitation as he had a good memory and 'presented' well. I was sometimes pressed into giving a recitation as well, something like Robert Service's *The Cremation of Sam McGee.* I would be hard pressed to recite it now.

Following the 'entertainment,' supper would be served. The obligation (privilege?) of providing the sandwiches and cake rotated and, as would be expected, there was a good deal of rivalry among the ladies to see who could provide the best fare. My turn came after my mother had died. I did not relish having to present my humble offerings, although by this time I had fairly well mastered bread making. My sandwiches were salmon; it was cheap then. As I offered them in a large container to the people seated on long benches around the perimeter of the classroom, I knew that my bread baking talent would be under review. As I approached one of our more crotchety neighbours the second time around, she remarked to me, "Bought the bread, did you?" I was taken aback. I had never bought a loaf of bread in my life. For one thing it would be much too expensive and would also show ineptitude on my part. "Oh no," I said, "I made it." I'm not sure she believed me, but it was a compliment, in a backhand sort of way.

The drinks served would be coffee and some tea, taken around in large blue enamelled jugs. The coffee at Ailsa Craig was made in the basement on a three-burner coal oil stove. A large copper boiler would be filled with water, a big cloth bag full of coffee added and the whole brought to a boil. The desks from upstairs had been stacked in a corner of the school basement, not far from the stove, the coats from the assemblage piled on the desks. Then the sleepy small children were laid to sleep on the coats. I wonder if it ever occurred to anyone what a dangerous practice it was. The open flames of the oil stove in conjunction with the proximity of the flammable clothing and the sleeping children made it a very real hazard. On top of that, there was only a single stairway exit. It was an invitation to disaster, which fortunately did not happen.

Some nights were special, such as the Pie Socials and the Box Socials. The boxes would be filled lovingly with a lunch for two. There was great rivalry, particularly among the single young women to make their box attractive and different; much ingenuity was used.

A cardboard shoe box was the favoured base and the adornments depended on taste and availability of decoration materials. The maker of each box was supposed to be a deep secret, but it was interesting how often the box went to the preferred buyer.

The Pie Socials operated on the same format as the Box Social but the pies were not ornamented. The auctioneer at Ailsa Craig was a young man of French Canadian extraction; he bore the exotic name Ulysses, which our English speaking community pronounced Ullis. In his own inimitable style, Ullis would auction off the boxes or pies at just the right speed, coaxing money from the young swains, money that would be used to cover expenses incurred for supplies and perhaps for the orchestra that provided the dance music.

For some boxes and pies the bidding would be hot and heavy as rivals for a young lady's affections would offer their all. It was watched with great interest, and amusement, by the elders. My pie making ability was almost nil, so I undertook to bake my particular pie with much trepidation. I chose an impossible filling, pineapple. No one had told me that pineapple does not make a good pie. On top of that, my crust was amateurish, to say the least. So the combination of an impossible filling and an almost disastrous crust arrived at the pie social. I knew who I wanted to buy it, and he did, Ralph Tyson. The runny filling and the hard crust did not deter him from eating a bit of it, but it certainly did nothing for my reputation as a pastry cook.

Ralph and I liked each other, which did not please my father. He and Ralph's father, John, had homesteaded near each other and their tobacco trail was legend. The tobacco trail was between the two farms, about a mile and a half, and the story was that when one or the other set out to borrow tobacco, nothing deterred them. They cut a straight path from one farmsite to the other, through sloughs and any other obstruction, to get the tobacco. After a few years, the Tysons moved to an adjoining district. During the dark days of the depression, when our phone had been disconnected, there was no means of direct communication.

One Friday winter evening Ralph had stopped at our house to take me to a dance. Alas, I was not home; I had gone with another young man who had come earlier. I had no intimation that Ralph would be calling for me, otherwise I would have been waiting. The interesting aspect to this little episode is that I never did know that

Ralph had called for me until years later when my aunt mentioned it in casual conversation. My father, who was at home when Ralph called, had 'neglected' to tell me.

When their families were young, John Tyson would taunt my father about having four girls while he, John, had four boys. My father retorted, "Never mind, John, on Sunday nights you will be milking the cows by yourself because your four boys will be at my place courting my four girls." Something happened along the way because no romantic connections were made. But Ralph and I came close. He never told me he had called and he took my absence as rejection. Sad, that a lack of communication can influence the tangent of one's life. Or maybe it was the dreadful pie!

Oh yes, about the dances. The foxtrot and the waltz were standard fare, sometimes the polka and the two-step, but the real favourites were the square dances. The square dance caller was always Ullis; his distinctive enunciation was a crowd pleaser; his talent was much sought after. There were usually three musicians: banjo, violin and piano being basic instruments. The Tyson family were standbys and always generous with their talent.

Once a year, the Glen Eagle school would host Burns Night. It was not a large school and the place would be packed by the large Scots community. Scottish dances would prevail, Strip-The-Willow being one of the favourites, and a good time guaranteed for all.

But even in that innocent time, there would be acts of vandalism. One Friday night, at the end of the evening, an elderly neighbour went to the barn to hitch his team to the sleigh for the journey home. He found, to his dismay, that his harness reins had been cut into pieces. When they were brought into the schoolhouse and displayed, we all felt chagrin and disgrace that something so hostile had occurred in our genial midst. The culprits were never determined, but many in the community had their suspicions: outsiders, of course.

Exhausted after a night of dancing and fun, we bundled into our heavy winter clothing and took the long sleigh ride home. There would be straw and blankets to give us some warmth, but the sound of the horses hooves on the hard snow, and their harness, especially if they wore bells, combined with the rocking motion of the sleigh, encouraged sleep. On a clear night, and most were clear, myriads of stars shone overhead. The star conscious would keep us awake by challenging us to point out the ones we could name. If the night sky was particularly generous, the northern lights would perform their magic; it was their turn to dance!

Finally, we would reach home where we lit a fire in the cold cookstove so we could heat the flatirons to warm our beds. Wrapped in a heavy towel, a flatiron held its heat for a long time. I found out how long one night after a dance; I awoke in the morning to find that my flatiron cover had slipped and the sharp point of the iron had burned a hole deep in my leg near the right shin bone. I have that scar to this day.

Paid Work

How often seemingly small things turn out to matter big! My future was determined by a spool of thread, or rather, by the cost of a spool of thread.

I was eighteen, my mother had been dead for three years. Lois, my next-younger sister, had just turned sixteen; it would soon be her turn to take over. It was the heart of the depression. We had no telephone; it had long since been cut off for lack of payment. An irony, because my father had been one of the main instigators in having the phone lines extended from Harris, sixteen miles into our part of the country. He had suggested that the lines be buried underground, but they had been strung on poles in the conventional manner. Had they been placed underground, it would have been a great saving in maintenance costs. I remember the day clearly, when two representatives of the phone company came to our farm and told us that we were losing the phone. It must have been a very low point in my father's life. On the pragmatic side, we probably would no longer have been able to afford the big cylindrical batteries required to operate it.

It was a late summer afternoon when the big car drove into our yard and a stranger inquired if this was the home of the Gifford girls? I was home and replied that it was. The year was 1934, the crop would be almost a complete failure, again there would be nothing to harvest. In those years, the seven years of the big drought, a farmer in Saskatchewan, at least in our part of the province, was lucky to get his seed back.

The stranger, who was accompanied by his wife, said our name had been given to them by someone who knew of our plight. He said he farmed down near Rosetown and that he and his wife were looking for someone to help over the harvest. Would I care to come? I would. They did not get out of their car, but apologized for calling without warning; they had not been able to phone. I said I understood.

As I would only be gone for two or three months, Lois could manage for that time. I put a few of my scant possessions together and went off in the big, black car on my first job where I would earn some money. The pay was not large, $7.00 a month. I earned my money, in spades.

The farm was a large one, even by Saskatchewan standards. It was not far from town; mechanized; without electricity, and maintained a sizable dairy herd of Jersey cattle. The Jersey bull, by the way, is considered to be the most dangerous of farm bulls because it does not close its eyes when it charges. The farm where I was to be employed was in a good agricultural belt that meant it had always enjoyed a marketable crop. I had moved into an environment that, while not luxurious, was certainly above my own.

The somewhat elderly couple had three children: a son "S", who worked on, and was the heir to the farm. His older sister had just obtained her first school teaching position some distance from her home. The youngest daughter was an invalid; she lived at home.

The lady of the house had suffered from arthritis for many years and her hands were so crippled from the disease, it was almost impossible for her to perform even simple tasks. I could see why they needed help. I soon learned the routine.

One of my tasks was making butter. Jersey cattle are noted for the richness of their milk so there was plenty of butter making to do; it had to be done right because it was marketed. The chore was done down in the milk-house, which gave me the benefit of being away from the critical demands of my employer. She maintained a special diet that was supposed to alleviate the effects of her arthritis. As the result of diet consciousness, the food that was prepared every day was far removed from the fare that I was used to. It required a good deal of preparation.

I did all of the household work: cooking, cleaning, washing and ironing. When the heavy load of harvest work was waning, I was told that it was time to wash the living room ceiling. That was bad news. The large living room, which I had never seen used, had heavy beams across the ceiling which was painted all over with flat white paint. Washing a ceiling is never easy, but when it was painted with flat paint that clung to the wash cloth, it was hard work, indeed. I found it worse than I had feared it would be; it took me days under observant supervision, so I couldn't cut corners. For me, working on that farm, being a servant, was a definitive sociological experience. I did not receive any time off, but I was given one appreciated privilege; I could use the sewing machine. As I desperately needed a decent housedress, I bought a length of cotton print on an evening when I was given permission to go into town with a neighbour. As I was leaving the house, my employer said to me, "Don't forget to buy the thread." Thread was five cents a spool and one of the sewing machine drawers contained spools of almost every common color. Five cents would not have made a dent in the family fortune. I was given an advance on my pay so I could buy the material and the thread.

Not long before the thread incident, the farmer had confided to me, one evening at the kitchen table when his wife was not there, that he had well over fifty thousand dollars in the bank. That amount placed him among the wealthy in the heart of the depression. If you save enough five cents, they add up: my Scottish extraction made me appreciate that. When the three months of my employment were finally over, I was paid my $21.00, less the advance for the yard goods and the thread.

I returned home to what seemed a strange land. Our living room was lived in. We did not religiously go to church every Sunday evening and sit in the exact same pew. Actually, we had no church to go to as the student ministers only came for a short while in the summer; the service was held in the schoolhouse. I returned to the rough and tumble of living with very lively siblings and a father who didn't seem to care what happened to us. I knew I would soon have to go. My older sister, Jean, had left not long after our mother died. Her explanation later, when my sister, Lois, chided her about it, was that she realized how hopeless our situation was, and the rest of us did not. Now it was my turn to go.

But I had made a conquest. The farmer's son missed me. He would drive the twenty-five miles in his truck to take me to school dances. It was rumoured through the district that Ina had a new boy friend, a wealthy farmer from Rosetown. But I had experienced the style of life of his family and knew that his wife would be helplessly absorbed. The spool of thread incident had been a good warning. I could have gotten even; I could have married their only son. But I did not, I turned him down.

It was a dreary mid-April day in 1935. I was nineteen when I took my last sleigh ride with my father, over fields that had scarcely enough snow to support the sleigh; an omen that it would be another bad year.

I was on my way to the city.

The Letter

I am reproducing here a letter that was written on February 29, 1916. It was sent to my grandmother Elder by her sister-in-law, Grandpa's sister, Ellen, who lived on the Elder family farm in Scotland. There was no love lost between the two women, and one can understand why: it was Ellen who persuaded her brother (my grandfather) to leave his eldest daughter, Agnes, with her. Ellen was a spinster and a very strong willed woman who bought the farm in 1916, the farm that the Elders had tilled as tenants since 1660!

But to get back to the letter: in the summer of 1980, I visited my Aunt Ettie Elder who was staying on the farm for part of the summer. In the course of checking the books from the Lady Minto Library which were kept in a shed adjoining the house, I noticed a small, black velvet drawstring bag hanging on a nail and asked my aunt what was in it; she did not know. On opening it, I found cotton thread knitting that my grandmother had been making; the unused thread was wound around a piece of paper. On examining it, I found the letter that is reproduced here.

Bents,
West Calder,
29. 2. 16

Dear Betsy.

Was so pleased to get your letter yesterday. Just thought I
would reply at once. We were wondering if anything was
wrong. When you did not write to Agnes at her birthday, I
could not tell you all the conjectures we had, thought some
of you must be ill or Isabel had not got through her trouble
aright (sic) and you were not there. She wrote Agnes and told
her they had got two new rooms added to their house and that
she was expecting. What will this ones name be? Agnes will
require to wait until the next one comes before she will get a
name. She won't be pleased when she sees this but it is just
in fun. She need not have taken up two first names with her
first girl seeing they are coming so fast. She would have got
one to call Jean now. It must have been very cold when your
very bread was frozen. I thought your menfolk would have
gotten common sense by this time, not to get more things to
work with than what were just required. I don't wonder you
feel annoyed, but talk to them and try and make them understand that life is too short for us to be selfish. And we all have
to try and do our bit in helping others that are not so well off.
In the photo we thought you all looked real nice, even the
view we got of the house, it seemed quite nice. Did we see
the door? There was a place we thought was the door but we
were not sure. Here wood is such a price that no one is buying
wood or repairing anything that can possibly stand over. And
the plantations that will do for pit wood are being cut down.
The one west side of Fernie is soon all cut. Mrs. Dick says you
can see right to Wilsontown now. The Farm has lost valuable
shelter, other woods on Hermand will soon follow it. We have
not ships to bring stuff-in to us, freight that used to be 12/6
a ton is now eight pounds, so I leave you to judge what prices
we are paying for our feeding for cows and pigs and hens.
I have 18 chickens out of 24 eggs, I am quite pleased at having
so many but have no more set. Snow is going away today
and it is raining, and such a slush. We had to send for Mr.

Bothwick yesterday, a horse had got a chill, her feet and legs have to be bathed today. So I am going away to help as soon as the water is warm. Agnes was asked to a tea party at West Calder yesterday after he got a cup of tea here. He motored her down to her spree altho it was off his road. He is not married yet, belongs to the good old *Pauline Order*. Next morning: Am sorry to say mare does not look any better at present but she may improve through the day. Frost again and more snow. They tell me in England snow is about a foot deep and wreaths are about 20 feet deep, so we won't get clear of snow until it is away there. Farm work is very far behind, we have a lot of ploughing to do yet and no garden work done. I had a letter from John Glay, Toronto, last week, he says the lumber trade is at a standstill as none is exported just now. I should think this was the time to get up your house as wood should be cheap but labour will likely be high. Yon would be your byre beside your barn and Bessie with her fine pony and trap, we cannot come upside with you. We had a Mr. Hodge from Brownhill near Carnwath the other week. At one time he had a fancy to go to Canada, but a cousin of his who had been out, and came home, told him it was Heaven for women but Hell for men and horse. I hear of no dispute about Mr. Mitchell's will, the Dr. said he was all right when he made it. Mr. Elder says she is a clever woman, he never saw anything wrong with her and she looked well after Mr. Mitchell's comfort. She comes from about Selkirk. The farm had to be kept for a year, trustees to pay rent. I trust this may reach you all right and find all well as we are living in a fearful time. Trusting to hear from you soon, I remain,

Yrs. H. Elder

In the letter, my great-aunt Ellen (Helen) had mentioned Isabel's 'trouble' which was then a euphemism for pregnancy. The trouble to which she was referring was me! I find this interesting from two standpoints: the mail service between Scotland and Canada in 1916 would be by vessel and rail, and the time factor shows that there was not much difference between the 1916 time and today's surface mail. And isn't it a delightful irony that a letter which had been written sixty-four years before, and had hung on that nail in that little bag for fifty years (my grandmother died in

1930), should be found by me, as though it had hung there waiting for me all those years.

The letter that my great-aunt addressed to Canada in 1916 is
informative, not so much for what it says as for what it does not
mention: the only reference to the 1914-18 Great War which was
raging at that time, is in a monetary context, "We have not ships
to bring stuff in to us, freight that used to be 12.6 a ton is now eight
pounds", and the cursory reference to 'living in a fearful time' at
the end of the letter. There is no indication of apprehension or
concern for those engaged in the conflict, as if it were totally outside their orbit. This 1916 letter, which reveals such a lack of concern, is in sharp contrast to my memories of 1938: when I walked
to my boarding house at 616 Bedford Road in Saskatoon for lunch
at noon, I would open the door to the sound of Adolf Hitler shouting invectives from the loudspeaker of the big cabinet radio that
stood in the corner of the living room. His tirade was in a language
I did not understand except for geographical references (such as
Sudetenland, which was annexed by Germany that year). There
was an overlay of English interpretation, but the prevailing
memory is that of the hysterical voice of Adolph Hitler. It was a
prelude to the 1939-45 Second World War in which all Canadians
would become participants, whether active or passive, whether we
wished it or not. We were the beneficiaries of day to day reports
by print and radio; there was no hiding from its immediacy. We
simply could not have the luxury of ignorant indifference such as
my great-aunt Ellen enjoyed in 1916.

In my between the wars growing-up experience in
Saskatchewan, the closest we got to acrimony was best exemplified
by the 'spite fence.' There was a real spite fence not far from us.
Naturally, before a spite fence is built, the relationship between
neighbours had to have deteriorated to a point beyond reconcil-
iation. It has been said that, human nature being what it is, one
in every ten persons will dislike us on sight. Nothing we can do
about it! That is an almost comforting thought: it removes any
onus on us to rationalize the dislike and to perhaps try to do something about it.

Obviously, those two farmers had been unfortunate enough to
have that invidious tenth person as a neighbour and the two lines
of barbed wire, with the few inches between them, were a concrete
demonstration that even the vaunted friendliness of the prairies

sometimes did not exist. There is a hint in the 1916 letter that my grandmother was sometimes less than happy with the decisions made by her men. I know of one thing that aggravated her: she said that every time they got a bit of money ahead, Grandpa bought more land. Grandma had a desire to see the Pacific ocean, but no, land came first; she never did get to see the Pacific and visit relatives who lived in Vancouver. I cannot imagine that she would have liked to live in the mountains. Prairie people became addicted to far horizons.

Solace

When the heart goes out of a home, the home falls apart. Ours certainly did after our mother died. Iris had been born October 23, 1931, and our mother died November 11 from what was commonly known as child-bed fever. There were no antibiotics then to counteract the disease which had spread largely through ignorance of basic hygiene. It is ironic that our mother safely delivered her first three children: Jean, 1914; myself, 1916; and Los, 1918; at home. No doctor was there to preside at my entry during a blizzard in January, and I never saw a doctor until my tonsils were removed when I was in my early twenties. My mother had Eva, 1920; Ted, 1922; and John, 1923; in a distant Saskatoon hospital. Then the smaller hospital in Rosetown was built only twenty-five miles away. It was what was termed a municipal hospital, supported from municipal taxes. My mother had gone to Rosetown close to what she thought was her delivery time and had stayed with friends until Iris's imminent arrival, well past the due date.

The hospital kept Iris in their nursery for a couple of weeks after our mother's death, then I went with Uncle Jim in his Model A Ford to bring her home. As the youngest, John, was already eight years old, I had had no recent practice in caring for a baby. So at the age of fifteen I was shown how to bathe and care for her by considerate nurses who had become very fond of their charge. I am sure they watched Iris go in my insecure arms with much misgiving.

As a matter of fact, I almost killed Iris on the way home. The November day was bitterly cold, as November in Saskatchewan can be, and I had taken several blankets to keep her warm. I sat in the back seat along with the baby, very conscious of my responsibility. I kept piling on the blankets so she would not be cold. When I finally took a tentative peek to see how the baby was, I found a little red face gasping for air. I had almost smothered her to death!

Our father was obsessed with the baby. As my sister, Lois, said to me in Vancouver, not many years ago, "Our father, as far as he was concerned, only had two children, Jean (the eldest) and Iris (the youngest)." But the burden of Iris's care fell on me. The hospital had given me a formula for her, the chief ingredient of which was a powder called Dextra Maltose. I was to phone the doctor in Harris, and regularly report her weight and condition. I weighed her by tying together the three corners of a triangular cloth diaper, placing the baby in this cradle and lifting the squirming bundle by the hook on an old spring scale that was used in the house for all weighing needs, accuracy not guaranteed.

She did well as fortunately she had been born a healthy child, nine pounds six ounces.

The baby was fine but our father was a different story; he simply went into retreat from all responsibility, so overwhelmed was he by his grief. At one point during the winter he went to visit distant friends and 'forgot' to return until a neighbour went for him and brought him back.

My mother and father had established a good marital relationship. Each had his or her sphere of influence and the other respected that; my mother was the one who carried the larger share: she set the rules of conduct and handled the family finances; she was the governing force in major decisions. At some point they had determined that when discipline was administered there would be no interference by the other partner.

Now, with her help and guidance gone, my father was adrift in a sea of uncertainty. He leaned on me. I was not yet sixteen but was expected to carry the load that had been my mother's. It is interesting that, when she had a presentiment that she would not survive her confinement, my father had asked, "Who will look after us?", and she had said, "Ina will." So my father laid the burden on me.

It was a burden I was finding increasingly intolerable. Three calamities had coincided: first, our mother's death; second, the long depression and third, a seven-year drought that brought desperation to even strong families.

The depression robbed us of money but the drought robbed us of food; I find that is a fact not generally recognized elsewhere in Canada; the double whammy that hit the prairies in the thirties.

On a hot July day when I was seventeen, I took the garden fork and went down to the garden to see if I could dig a few potatoes for supper. I was alone. Without warning, a feeling of helplessness overwhelmed me and, as I tried to dig in the hard soil for pitifully small potatoes, I began to cry, something I rarely did. Tears poured from me, tears so large they splashed on the handle of the fork. I cried and cried, imprisoned by cares from which there was no escape, and the awful fear that the long drought would never be over. I continued crying as I carried my meager harvest back to the kitchen and prepared to wash the potatoes in a white enamel basin on the kitchen table.

As I put my hands in the water they both froze to the bottom of the basin and I blacked out, became unaware of my surroundings. A soft, gentle voice spoke to me and said, "Heaven and Earth shall pass away but My Words shall not pass away." (ST. MATTHEW 24:35)

Then I was back, alone again, in the kitchen. I do not know why that particular verse from the Bible was said to me, but I do know that I never again reached the depth of despondency I felt that day.

I was given strength to carry my burdens.

At Last!

As the team of horses pulling the sleigh zig-zagged their way across the open field, from snow patch to snow patch, in early April, 1935, the last journey was being taken; I was leaving home. I had no regrets, only anticipation. My father was taking me down to John Tyson's. I would spend the night there before going into the town of Harris, where I would board the CNR train for Saskatoon.

My father and I did not speak of what lay ahead; he offered no

advice though he had been a worldly young man when he came
west from Boston to his homestead twenty six years before.

I do not remember what kind of luggage I carried, but it would
not be large as I had scarcely anything to take; just a few garments
I had made myself on the old treadle sewing machine, using material purchased from my earnings for the three months I worked on
the big farm at Rosetown during the 1934 harvest. There would be
precious little harvest on the Gifford farm for 1935; the paucity
of snow on the field we were crossing boded ill for any kind of
yield. The five years of drought we had just endured had taught
us that it was probably folly to expect rain. The Biblical 'Seven years
of drought' were seemingly being fulfilled. But now I, at least,
would be free, free of responsibility toward my five younger siblings. Now it was Lois's turn to take over; Lois was at last old
enough, she had turned sixteen in October.

I was going to Saskatoon, to business school with money Aunt
Ettie had loaned me, sixty dollars, fifty of that for tuition and the
balance to sustain me over the duration of the four-month course
at the Scott Business College. But there was a proviso to Aunt
Ettie's loan: that when I was through the course and earning
money, I would spend the sixty dollars to help my younger sister,
Eva, get started. The same arrangement had been made with Jean,
who had gone to Saskatoon a year before, after working in Harris,
and who had taken a business course at Scott's. She had agreed
that she would help Lois when the time came. By the time Lois,
and then Eva, left the farm and Jean and I had helped them as
agreed, Aunt Ettie changed her mind and said that the money did
not need to be repaid. But at least Jean and I had the satisfaction
of having taken care of our end of the bargain.

Jean had made arrangements for me to take care of the Scott
household while Mrs. Scott and the two young boys were away for
the summer. The Scotts lived in a three-storey house on Avenue H,
owned by a family named Kreutzweiser. Lloyd K., who worked for
the City of Saskatoon, shared the house with the Scotts. After my
arduous work on the farm, taking care of a city house, and the minimal amount of cooking, was not onerous. I went to the Scott Business College for both the daytime and night classes. Alas, I was not
a good student; my fingers did not have the dexterity to handle
the stiff manual typewriters with ease, nor did my fingers travel
across the lines of my shorthand book at the required precision and

speed. I tried hard, but obviously, I was not in my natural element.

The summer dragged on; I saw little of Jean, she was busy with her own endeavours, and she and I had never enjoyed a close rapport.

Mrs. Scott would be returning soon to take over her household; my help would not be required. It was time to think seriously about getting a job, an almost impossible undertaking for someone with minimal talent and no clout. I was naive to the point of embarrassment, a waif in homemade clothes, with one pair of shoes, ugly black oxfords, knowing nothing of the city and its ways... hopeless, absolutely hopeless, especially in the hopeless year, 1935. I learned the desperation of my situation in a hurry as I trudged the streets of Saskatoon.

I went in and out of every business on Second Avenue, the main business street... nothing, nothing at all. I did the same on all the other streets and avenues, receiving the shake of the head everywhere. I remember that when I went into the Speers Seed Company. Mrs. Speers, an older woman, greeted me. When she learned that I was John Elder's granddaughter from Harris, she spoke highly of my grandparents who had been good customers at Speers Seed. So when she shook her head and said they had no work for me, there were tears in her eyes.

Time was running out for me, only the thought of having to return to the hated farm drove me on. As I stood one day at the corner of Second Avenue and Twenty First Street, I noticed a big sign above the Great Western Furniture store entrance proclaiming that they were having a sale. I reasoned that if they were having a sale, they might need some extra help. When I went in to enquire, about noon, I was told to see a Mr. Cowan after he had returned from lunch. Oh joy! While I waited, I wandered through the store, getting the feel of it. I had time to explore all three floors. I saw fine chesterfields, chairs, tables, coffee tables and other beautiful case goods on the main floor; large dining room sets, bedroom suites and hope chests on the second with lower priced studio lounges and kitchen sets on the lower. There was a large drapery section on the main floor and a workroom at the back where women at electric sewing machines fashioned stylish slip covers for upholstered goods. It was a magical place and I longed to be part of it.

When Mr. Cowan returned from lunch, many duties awaited him. He was the secretary treasurer of the company, and the

onerous job of interviewing personnel had been foisted off on
him; he had little stomach for it. I was just another waif looking
for work, but he was kind enough to listen patiently as I spun my
tale of woe, scarcely stopping for a deep breath. It was my big
chance and I was not going to let go of it!

I think he was sorry for me, how could he not be? A motherless
child with five younger brothers and sisters at home and nothing
but rejection ahead. He did not ask me to demonstrate my abili-
ties (a good thing!), but told me to report for work in the office,
Monday, September 23rd.

Forty years after, in my Uncle John's deserted farm shack, I found
a calendar, hanging on the wall, and there it was, perfectly preserved, September, 1935, showing a picture of Twenty First Street
in Saskatoon, with the Great Western Furniture on the south side
of the street and the imposing Bessborough Hotel, which opened
in 1935, at the far end. I have that calendar page, framed; it was
as though it had been kept just for me.

I started off at my first job badly. The typewriter I was assigned
was a heavy old machine with right-hand throw. It was an absolute
killer. The muscles of my right arm ached as I used it, and after.
Or tried to use it. Mr. John Hair, the President of the Great Western Furniture, spent a whole afternoon dictating collection letters to me. I was so nervous, I could hardly discern what he was
saying, let alone get it down accurately in my pathetic attempt at
shorthand.

But I plowed ahead, fighting the cursed machine, and fighting
my inability to make sense of the shorthand. It was all just too
much. There was no one in the office who gave me any help, even
sympathy. The return to the farm loomed in the background. What
could I do?

I had found a boarding house within walking distance of downtown. It was a rangey three-storey house run by what was then
known as a grass widow, a woman who was separated from her husband. She had two school age boys and was raising them alone. Her
last name was Carson, and the residents of the house referred to
it as The Carsonage. My place in the scheme of things there was
somewhere between that of boarder and domestic help. The $30.00
per month that I was paid by The Great Western Furniture Company was not sufficient to allow me to pay full board, so I had
undertaken to pay $18.00 per month and work off the balance. I

worked in the kitchen, washing dishes for the many boarders, eating in the kitchen with the boys and doing whatever Mrs. Carson required of me. I received a letter from my father asking if I could send him $5.00 a month; I had to reply that I could not, after all, I had scarcely a decent stitch of clothes to my name.

But my real moment of stress lay ahead: one of the boarders came down with scarlet fever. At that time, quarantine for communicable diseases was compulsory; the residents of the Carsonage would not be allowed to leave the premises for (I cannot recall the exact time, but it was lengthy). A notice attached to the front door verified the quarantine.

I was in a state of near panic. I phoned the office to advise them that I would not be available for some time. After I remembered that a fellow student at Scott's was still looking for work, I called back to the GWF to tell Mr. Cowan that I knew someone who would fill in for me, his reply, "Oh, it has been taken care of." So fast! Mrs. Carson took advantage of the situation by directing me to wash all the white woodwork, of which there was a substantial amount. Being confined did not affect my social life; I had none. A school teacher and her university student son boarded at the Carsonage; he asked his mother if he could take me to a university function. She told him he could not and went to the function with him herself. I accepted the rejection with equanimity. After all, I had nothing to wear!

We were released, finally, from quarantine a day earlier than anticipated so I went down to the office. It was noon hour, almost everyone was at lunch. I went right to my desk; a beautifully composed letter was beside the typewriter. I picked it up and looked at the initials of the typist: "AB". My heart fell. A student in my class at Scotts had been an Amy Boyce; I didn't understand why she was taking it, she was so talented. If Amy Boyce was my fill-in, obviously against her I did not stand a chance! It was Amy Boyce.

I don't know what saved my job, certainly not talent, maybe dedication, or just plain luck. My five years at the GWF were a hard apprenticeship. Mr. John Hair, who had been the mayor of Saskatoon, had a work ethic that would dismay any employee.

No matter what you did, or how you did it, it was wrong because then you would do it better the next time. That, combined with the GWF reputation for "All work and no pay" almost broke my spirit. But at Christmas, I enjoyed real spirits for the first time! All

of the GWF staff gathered on the lower level for a dash of con-
viviality or two. I participated: I accepted whatever I was offered!
Mr. Hair's wife, a regal Scot who could easily be envisioned as the
mayor's consort, could see where things were heading. She spoke
to me quietly, when the occasion offered, with words of wisdom:
"Ina, it is not wise to mix your drinks." I have never forgotten that
kind admonition, for the simple reason it showed that someone
cared. It was as though my mother had spoken.

I almost cried.